A Fragrant Fullness

A Fragrant Fullness

Ambassador Emerald International
427 Wade Hampton Boulevard
Greenville, S.C. 29609 U.S.A.
and

Ambassador Productions Ltd.
Providence House
Ardenlee Street
Belfast BT6 8QJ, Northern Ireland

www.emeraldhouse.com

Cover design and page layout by A & E Media, Sam Laterza

ISBN 1 889893 90 0

The Spiritual Essence of Everyday Life

A Fragrant Fullness

Marsha Maurer

AMBASSADOR
EMERALD INTERNATIONAL

GREENVILLE, SOUTH CAROLINA • BELFAST, NORTHERN IRELAND
www.emeraldhouse.com

Acknowledgements

The author extends her sincerest gratitude to all those who have contributed to this work, including my husband Michael for his enduring love and support; Norma Schmelling for the inspiration of her perennial correspondence; Pegge Schall and Ashley Futeral of House of Versailles Perfumery in Charleston, South Carolina for prompting me to pursue my interest in fragrance; Our Redeemer Lutheran Ladies A. M. Bible Study for sharing their Scriptural insights; Rev. Karl J. Dunker for generating questions and facilitating answers; Joe Thomas for his friendship and introduction to Southern nature; Augusta State University's Reese Library staff for their pleasant and valuable assistance; my family, Al and Maxine Junghans, Jolene and Earl Stackhouse, Gary and LaDonna Junghans, and Lesa Wunder, for their persistent encouragement; Kirk Moore and Don Fry of Quiet Pond in Augusta, Georgia for personal library loans and fond collaboration; readers of *In the Garden: A Collection of Prayers for Everyday*, for their heartfelt and enthusiastic responses; and Tomm Knutson an d the staff of Ambassador Emerald, International for their talented attentions to *A Fragrant Fullness*.

Dedication

*With love and gratitude to my dear husband Michael,
who infuses our marriage with savor and significance.*

"I wish that life should not be cheap, but sacred,
I wish the days to be as centuries, loaded, fragrant."
Ralph Waldo Emerson

"In thy presence is fullness of joy."
Psalm 16:11 (KJV)

Introduction

No doubt my fondness for scent was instilled by my mother's enchanting roses and peonies, my father's cherry blend pipe tobacco, and my grandfather's dill at dusk. To me as a child, whether hanging family laundry to dry, rolling down the grassy knoll beside my grandfather's strawberry patch, watching the cosmetician blend face powder in Cole's Department Store, or opening September textbooks, scent always distinguished the experience.

While my husband Michael and I lived and traveled in Europe during his military career, fresh farm produce from village markets and adventuresome dining piqued our interest in European herbs, inspiring our experimental approach to cooking. We savored morels only hours from the forest floor, country tortes topped with strawberries and clouds of cream from a farmyard cow, and subtle chervil soup of garden herbs in the hills. We enjoyed a supper of boiled eggs, fresh spinach, and earthy potatoes with nuns of a hill-top convent, heard their voices raised in vespers, then burrowed beneath down-filled comforters as a sublime storm crashed about our ancient tree-top perch. When we settled into our first home after my husband's retirement, he responded to my long-held desire by building a culinary herb garden, which has provided us endless pleasure.

We have learned about gardening and the South, just as we have learned about every other new terrain, by immersion. In colorful vernacular, we have been reassured that Southerners are as unfamiliar with the Midwest as we were with their realm. "All I know about Kansas," one local remarked, "is some ol' gal bumped her head on the bed, lost her slippers, and had that dumb dog named Dodo." Could I help it that I laughed aloud?

On another occasion, the facilitator of a university book discussion about Frank Baum's *The Wizard of Oz* expressed incredulity that anyone would want to return to the bleakness of Kansas. When I could not refrain from setting the record straight about the state's true nature, she responded with the most astonished expression: "I have never met ANYONE from KANSAS!" as though it were Pluto. Shortly thereafter, I was struck by the incongruity of the ice cream wagon which prowled our neighborhood playing "Home on the Range." While crossing state borders does not require us to carry passports, foreign currency, or a pocket dictionary, I have been reminded just how expansive our country is and how intriguingly foreign its own distinct regions.

I hope that recognition will transcend the personal sense of place and experience in the following pages, inspiring readers to explore their own spiritual territories. In fragrant reflection, may readers savor the fullness of joy with which God's presence imbues our world and sanctifies our lives.

Fragrance by Design

*F*ragrance is my lodestar in the garden. Scent, rather than color, is the principal criterion I apply in making garden selections. And since many fragrant plants, shrubs, and vines are often white blossoming, my husband and I have created an almost entirely white and green garden in varying shades—deep, pale, bluish, and chartreuse greens; bright, transparent, and opalescent whites—which appeal to the sense of tranquility we desire in a garden. I also rely on shape and texture for visual interest—fernlike, lacy, spiked, sprawling, and mounded variations. When considering height and shape of landscaping, nearly any size fragrant plant can be found, from tall trees to miniature ground covers.

But selecting plants by scent does pose challenges. To begin with, nursery personnel are seldom versed in the knowledge or vocabulary of fragrance. The landscaping original to our home was selected exclusively by size and shape. Scent, a common omission, was never considered in its design. At garden centers, I have been discouraged by a focus on color which frequently limits fragrant selections, and disappointed by unscented plants labeled as scented varieties. Directions for growing fragrant plants have often been lacking as well. And I have heard the descriptor "sweet" applied indiscriminately to citrusy, spicy, musky, and rosy essences and everything in between.

But a little research is worth the effort to create fragrant outdoor spaces. To begin with, scented plants are best enjoyed when air is quiet or breeze is faint. An enclosed area or protected spot will capture fragrance and keep strong winds from carrying it away.

Unlike bright splashes of color, fragrance can seldom be enjoyed at a distance, so plantings are best situated where their nectars can be detected. On pathways, scents can be released when crushed underfoot or savored as they are brushed in passing. Flowering vines on trellises and arbors climb skyward, reaching for a little heaven to pull it nearer, in drifts of what medieval gardeners described as God's breath on earth. Perfumed pots on steps or near doorways provide fragrant greetings. A patch of miniature gardenias sweeten the arrival of guests at the base of our front stairs. Jasmine covering a privacy screen near our kitchen windows transports me from washing dishes. Window boxes can invite aromas indoors as well.

Selection should also consider where time is spent and when fragrance is released. Near our bedroom window, an evergreen clematis blooms just as spring's open-window weather begins. Night-bloomers are especially appropriate near a bedroom window or on a patio where evenings are enjoyed. On our terrace wall, moon vines begin to unfold their sublime allure at dusk. Plants which release their scent after rain might work well near a fountain. And a winter-blooming daphne would obviously be best situated near a door, or perhaps a mailbox, when cold weather limits outdoor forays.

Whether we love lavish color, collect iris specimens, or specialize in vegetables, every garden plot benefits from some fundamental principle to provide coherence. For Christians, it is God's love which gives our lives direction and concord. We find guidance in Ephesians 5:2: "Live a life of love, just as Christ loved us and gave himself up for us as a fragrant offering and sacrifice to God." Reminding us of His grand design, God indicates appropriate choices, resolves our conflicts between the allures of this world and our spiritual welfare, assists us in recognizing our strengths, and helps us to select worthy priorities. He will guide our lives toward a harmonious wholeness.

Speaking of Scent

How would you describe the scent of your husband or granddaughter or cat? of toast? of old newspapers? of new-mown grass? You might begin by comparing the smell to something we would recognize. It is like baby powder or hay, or it is spicy, burnt, or inky, but such terms presume we are familiar with what is being compared. You might use adjectives for the scent's effect on us—intriguing, appealing, or repellent, but those who smell it may respond differently. Even words like tangy, cloying, pungent, foul, or putrid can encompass a wide range of scents.

Although we can easily detect even slight variations among odors, verbally discriminating among scents is difficult because our vocabulary for smell is imprecise. Nuances of color are easily articulated. Red may be cardinal, carmine, cerise, cherry, crimson, maroon, rose, ruby, scarlet, vermilion, or wine. But such distinctions are impossible for odors. Even garden catalogues describe fragrant plants in less than specific terms by relying on such limited language as intense, delicious, delicate, delightful, sweet, or fresh, repeated for plants with greatly distinct aromas. Ordering from such inadequate descriptions is completely guesswork.

Fortunately, we need not wonder about spiritual terminology. God speaks to us clearly. His word conveys an accurate account of His love for His people, His law, His grace, His promises. He leaves no doubt about how we are to live and, because we fail, what He has done to redeem us. "For God so loved the world that He gave his one and only Son, that whoever believes in him shall not perish but have eternal life" (John 3:16). The more we study His words, the more easily we discern His will, His wisdom, and His effusive goodness.

Moonlit Embrace

*W*hen the air cools, fireflies begin to flitter, and the heavens shimmer with stars, a fragrant intensity often suffuses the evening garden. Perhaps because our sense of sight is dimmed, we become more susceptible to the intimate charms of scent. In addition, many night bloomers use their nectars to lure night-feeding insects and moths which navigate by smell. White blossoms, silver foliage, and evening fragrance are essentials of a moonlight garden. The pale colors reflect light and focus attention on the garden's shapes and textures, and extravagant scents permeate the dark.

Fragrant flowers which make delicious additions to the evening garden include evening primrose, phlox, pinks, night-blooming jasmine, night-scented stock, sweet autumn clematis, nicotiana, and white sweet rocket, known as vesper flower. Artemesia, lamb's ears, wormwood, lavender, or any silver-leafed or woolly gray plants add textural interest and luminescence. Local nursery professionals can suggest choices which are appropriate to individual growing conditions.

One of our favorite evening enchantresses is the moon vine. My husband soaks the hard seeds for two days, then patiently scratches a tiny hole in the shell of each before starting them in potting soil. When seedlings have grown their third set of leaves, he plants them near our terrace wall. Large, heart-shaped leaves create a lush background for our herb garden during the day, and at dusk, a profusion of tightly twisted blossoms begin to dance, slowly unfurling their lemony invitation in a sashay of dazzling skirts.

When our private worlds are at their darkest, in times of discouragement, loss, despair, God's heavenly light still reflects on us, highlighting the positive, showing us how good can emerge from shadows.

In the dimmest hours—when a hurt is so deep we can't seem to overcome it, when health is assaulted and recovery seems distant, when a personal loss has left an gaping hole inside—God envelopes us in His fragrant presence and embraces us with His assurance of help. Numbers 6:24-26 promises His comfort, like a shimmer of moonlight in the dark: "The Lord bless you and keep you; the Lord make his face shine upon you and be gracious to you; the Lord turn his face toward you and give you peace."

Portable Perfume

One of the most intoxicating flowers I have been introduced to in the South is the ginger lily, which a friend brought to me with get-well wishes. A single small blossom scented the entire room and sent me on a determined quest to acquire these exquisite exotics for our own garden. Serendipitously, a neighbor came bearing a bundle of roots from a bunch of ginger lilies she had separated. She tells me she grows hers in a pot on a wheeled base so she can move the confection near her chair wherever she chooses to sit.

I love this idea of taking scent with us wherever we go. In effect, we do this ourselves by the attitudes we convey. Our outlook on life can emit a joyful essence which attracts others, or the rank odor of grumbling discontent and sullen bitterness, which is likely to make us undesirable company. The distinction is a conscious choice.

One of those unscientific magazine surveys once reported that above all else, even before love, security, and health, Americans claim to place greatest value on the absence of aggravation. I had to reread the results. Aggravation has always plagued us, from sin's arrival at the beginning of time, so why does it seem so insurmountable today? Perhaps it has to do with self-absorption. When we face our tasks and relationships as though they are unpleasant demands, begrudging our diverted attentions, we are, in effect, giving our own needs and desires priority. Our exasperated response to minor interruptions, inconveniences, and annoyances perpetuates our irritability. We grow impatient, we behave unkindly, we snap, or swear, or simmer. Often, agitation could be salved by stepping briefly outside ourselves for a moment to help someone, wait a turn, confront a problem, or complete a quick distasteful chore, all matters of attitude.

How can some people who have endured considerable heartache and hardship still waft a pleasant aura? They cultivate patience. They bear the balm of compassion and genuine interest in others. They squelch prejudice and grudges. They overlook imperfections and small slights. A familiar adage reminds us that "Forgiveness is the fragrance the violet sheds on the heel that crushed it." And the benefits of a cheerful disposition return to us. As the proverb goes, "Flowers leave some of their fragrance in the hand that bestows them." On our worst days, if we can extend bouquets beyond ourselves, we soon find we, too, are feeling better.

Followers of Christ convey the fragrance of His love. Others know His goodness by its manifestation in us. Henry Ward Beecher wrote, "A man ought to carry himself in the world as an orange tree would if it could walk up and down in the garden, swinging perfume from every little censor it holds up in the air." Because the scent of our actions and influence is often transported in ways and to places we cannot know, we want to conduct our lives in ways that please God, rather than simply following our own noses. As II Corinthians 2:14-15 reminds us, "Thanks be to God, who always leads us in triumphal procession in Christ and through us spreads everywhere the fragrance of the knowledge of him. For we are unto God the aroma of Christ."

Ephemeral Pleasures

*O*ur friend exclaimed, "Tonight is the night!" Eagerly anticipating the long-awaited event, he invited us to join him for the spectacle. We caught his contagious excitement as we sat in the evening air, exchanging stories, enjoying the song of tree frogs, checking often to see how soon the moment would arrive.

He called it, appropriately, the "ugly plant." Flat, rubbery stems and brown, aerial roots sprawled out of the pot in every direction, like limbs of a gangly adolescent. It had no form or shape about it, just wildly divergent stems and spidery roots in an imbalanced jumble. Downward growing buds had begun to point upward, indicating their imminent bloom.

"Just wait!" our friend promised. And so we did. Gradually we saw the blossom quiver, then, as if in time-lapse photography, begin to open its creamy white trumpet with reverberant notes of exquisite fragrance. With excruciating deliberation, the petals of the night-blooming cereus* began to flower on a star-burst background.

Yawning, eyelids drooping, with thoughts of rising early for the workday ahead, we lasted as long as we were able, pleased to have enjoyed the beginning of the revelation, expressed our regrets, and headed home.

The following day, our friend's excitement could not be contained. "You should have seen it!" He described the spectacular climax of the night-blooming cereus, which had reached its luxuriously fragrant perfection after midnight. Breathtaking blooms had revealed what our friend described as a "cathedral" of yellow stamens. And we had missed the grandeur. The blossom, which begins at dark, quickly withers at dawn.

In the garden, the most treasured moments are often the most fleeting—the moon vines which unfold their lemony fragrance for just an evening, the refreshing rain shower that quickly passes, the brilliant sunset that too soon disappears beyond the horizon. Similarly, in our lives, children grow up, health can become impaired, dear ones pass away. The greatest pleasures of this world quickly escape us while we are busy occupying ourselves with the trivial pursuits that crowd our days. Henry David Thoreau defines in *Walden* a more appropriate measure of satisfaction: "If the day and night are such that you greet them with joy, and life emits a fragrance like sweet-scented herbs, is more elastic, more starry, more immortal,—that is your success."

When Jesus visited his friends in Bethany, Martha scurried about making sure her guest was comfortable and well-fed while Mary quietly listened to Jesus talk. Although Martha grew frazzled because her sister was not helping, Jesus reminded her, "Martha, Martha, you are worried and upset about many things, but only one thing is needed. Mary has chosen what is better, and it will not be taken away from her" (Luke 10:41-42). In the frenzy of our own lives, we might recall those words which direct us to seek spiritual tranquility.

A fragrant garden can invite spiritual reflection by allowing us to sense God's serene presence, as Alexander Smith describes: "My garden with its silence and pulses of fragrance that come and go on the airy undulations, affects me like sweet music. Care stops at the gates, and gazes at me wistfully through the bars."

Moments in the garden remind us to slow down and enjoy the profound pleasures of the everyday and commonplace—to contemplate the rich variety of our blessings. God gives us immeasurable delights in this earth and in our lives. Living meaningfully means fully savoring the treasures we are given in our relationships with this world, with each other, and with our God.

* (Also called Queen of the Night, Nictocereus serpentinus is not actually a member of the cereus family.)

The Ides of March

I'd love a bigger garden than

The one I had last year;

I'd like the windows washed next week,

And woodwork done in here;

I'd much prefer wallpaper there,

And curtains fresh with starch:

Shakespeare was right when he advised,

Beware the "I'd's" of March.

I regret that I am unable to locate the original source of this poem, "Great Caesar's Ghost!" by Mary Margaret De Angelis, as I have it only as a little clipping torn out of a women's magazine and sent to me by my mother years ago. But its rereading always suggests to me the end of winter inertia and a spring full of enthusiasm and incentive ahead. We can identify with the poet's ambitions for the season's housekeeping, redecorating, and gardening and imagine the bright scents of furniture polish, starched curtains, and early blooms. Nurseries display their irresistible selections, and we begin to imagine opulent gardens drenched with fragrance. We forget how our enthusiasm can erode in midsummer battles with heat, drought, weeds, and vermin.

In our initial years of gardening, we scattered pots of blossoms about the terrace, on walls, down stairways, with generous abandon. Later we learned the challenges of keeping those flowers thriving through long Southern summers. We weighed their worth against our other interests and pursuits. We learned our limitations and priorities. Now we keep only a few low-maintenance pots and a small herb and vegetable garden.

Why do we often acknowledge our limitations so slowly? We want to be able to do it all. We feel driven to be productive, busy, successful, although we may not be sure why. And in the process, we may be ignoring what truly matters.

Even when we feel ourselves becoming tired, overwhelmed, and irritable, we find it difficult to accede to such human constraints as time, health, age, and resources, which restrict for each of us how much we can do and how well we can do it. Rather than rail against limitations, we would do well to recognize the benefits of restraint. These constraints actually help us establish priorities by reducing the choices available to us. They keep us focused on the precious present and on our invaluable relationships. They make us more patient, attentive, reflective, and peaceful. And isn't serenity just what we are yearning for? God's promises in Psalm 37:4, "Delight yourself in the Lord and he will give you the desires of your heart."

Bouquets of Thoughtfulness

May Day always brings nostalgic thoughts of May baskets. My fondest recollection of them is the beautiful blue and yellow construction paper cone, decorated with tissue streamers, filled with irresistible whiffs of jonquils, tulips, lilacs, and candy, left hanging on our door the morning of my youngest sister's birth—the gift, I later recognized, of our beloved aunt and uncle, who thoughtfully remembered three youngsters at home when our parents' presence and attentions were engaged by a new baby.

As children, in subsequent years, we designed hand-crafted baskets, often milk carton bottoms covered in construction paper, or berry baskets and tissue, to which we affixed ribbon handles and streamers, filled with garden flowers in bloom, confections, or cookies. Mother helped us make deliveries. We ran to the front doors of teachers, classmates, aunts and uncles, cousins, or neighbors of whom we were fond, rang the doorbell, and darted away so as not to be detected. The delight of May baskets is anonymity and surprise!

Usually when I mention to others this fond childhood tradition, responses intimate tepid appraisal of the quaint, outmoded practice. Perhaps it is for just this reason that I hold the spring holiday in esteem. It has not been appropriated by greeting card companies and retail emporiums to be permuted into an unrecognizable commercial extravaganza. Contrasted with the ghoulish greed of Halloween, for instance, the focus of May Day remains the simple virtue of thoughtfulness. The pleasure of bringing in the May is in giving it away.

The fact that May Day is seldom remembered in this homespun fashion does not daunt me. I still hang occasional May baskets on the doors of friends with a personal greeting. For youngsters or those who might be interested, I may enclose a simple history describing how young people in earlier times brought flowers or budding branches inviting friends to join May Day celebrations, and how this gesture evolved into the hanging of May baskets to show affection.

Hanging May baskets will probably never get much attention, which is precisely what gives these anonymous personal gestures of thoughtfulness meaning. It would be disappointing to find ready-made May baskets at a retail store, wouldn't it?

Sending flowers at other times to the sick, shut-in, hospitalized, lonely, or mourning is a common practice for good reason. Long after a card has been read, a visitor has left, or a phone call has ended, the kindness of the gesture remains in the beauty and bouquet of a garden greeting. The floral gift continues to convey compassion and concern as it scents a room. It need not be an exquisitely expensive arrangement. Often the most personal sentiments are expressed in a bunch of flowers, herbs, leaves, or branches from the garden in a simple container tied with a bright ribbon.

My mother inspires me. Even before breakfast, she can be found with a garden hose in her hand, mud on her shoes, seeds in her pockets, sun on her arms, breeze through her hair, and pollen on her nose, nurturing or collecting flowers for the church, shut-ins, and sundry occasions. Sharing her blossoms, she contributes to worship and offers welcome, sunny company.

When such expressions can so effectively lift spirits, why not deliver fragrant favors more often? A commonplace kindness can be profoundly savory: an attentive and sympathetic ear when a friend simply needs to talk, the squeeze of a hand or a hug when a family member yearns for a physical touch, a willingness to discuss the problem a spouse can't seem to resolve alone, an offer of help when a task is beyond a co-worker's capability.

Such freely offered indulgence is a true grace. Being "devoted to one another in brotherly love," as Romans 12:9 counsels, means shifting our focus from ourselves to recognize the need of another, then offering ourselves patiently, selflessly, unconditionally. This spirit of kindness is worth practicing all year. Whom might we delight today with a bouquet of thoughtfulness?

(Recently, I have encountered another old May Day tradition with spiritual connotations which may also be worth reviving, fastening a green sprig to the doorway with prayers of blessing for the home.)

Resonant Reverence

*S*easons and occasions of the church are marked not only by changes in vestments and liturgy, but also with varied natural expressions in the sanctuary. At Christmas time, the bright balm of evergreen trees and greens extol the birth of Jesus. Flanks of redolent lilies proclaim the excitement of the resurrection. In another beautiful Easter custom, members of our church insert spring blossoms from their gardens into a wire-covered, cross-shaped form for "the flowering of the cross," reminding worshipers that the risen Christ thransformed the instrument of His death into a symbol of life.

Marriage vows are often wafted on the scent of roses and other wedding flowers. Mourners express their sympathy with fragrant floral elegies. Bringing nature into church is nothing new. In medieval monastery gardens, monks cultivated herbs and vegetables, while nuns provided flowers to adorn sanctuaries and schooled ladies in the use of medicinal herbs and flowers. In England during Shakespeare's time, pews were strewn with sweet-scented flowers and lavender.

I Chronicles 16:29 encourages us to "Give unto the Lord the glory due unto his name: bring an offering, and come before him: worship the Lord in the beauty of holiness" (KJV). What better way to express our devotion than with the grace notes of God's own creation. Singing with resonant scent, these natural choirs suffuse our worship with reverence and breathe God's benediction.

Lasting Lilacs

When cowboys returned dusty, dirty, and exhausted from a long round-up, they were frequently soothed by lingering soaks in the bath and effusive splashing of lilac water. While men today would likely be embarrassed by so powerfully floral a fragrance, the provocative pleasure of lilacs is lasting, their scented sentiment indelible. In the rural Midwest, near crumbling foundations, they often remain to mark early homesteads, emitting the essence of families once intoxicated by screen door breezes. My own affection for lilacs derives from memory of their pale purple profusion in a fond aunt's back yard, arms full of aromatic amethyst.

In the shivering months of late winter, it is difficult to imagine the spindly, battered branches will ever flower. Yet, as sunlight brightens, weather-torn limbs are revived in the rays' warm return, coaxed back to life, and soon in rousing bloom. Likewise, we who believe in God's promise will survive our cold season in this world, even the dark void of death, to be restored to life in God's radiant presence. The intense aroma of lilacs exudes potent evidence of God's invincible power.

Peony's Promise

Although the peony is not distinguished by the opulent scent of some of my garden favorites, I cherish it for the profusion of memory it holds. Legend suggests that the plant's name honors Paeon, physician to the gods, who stanched wounds with a thickening milk from its healing root. A "paean" also refers to a laudatory hymn, tribute which seems appropriate to the peony's praiseworthy exuberance.

Great bobbing heads of peonies often bloom in Midwestern graveyards around Memorial Day, transplanted from family gardens to graves of loved ones. These heirloom plants are the legacy of pioneers who brought the esteemed plants west with them in covered wagons.

I like to think of their blossoms' most popular colors as stages of life: the creamy white innocence of infancy, the pale blush of youth, the vivid pink of active prime, and the deep wine of contemplative age. Once established, little seems to threaten peonies. They survive severe cold and drought; even foraging deer and rabbits avoid their bitter leaves. The stalwart plants endure, returning year after year for generations. My mother nurtures this sense of continuity, enjoying peonies from family graves rooted in her own garden. After their disappearance each fall, the crimson shoots reassuringly emerge the following spring with the rapid growth of extravagant leaves, ample buds, and abundant blossoms. Such voluptuous appearance contrasts with their demure perfume. Most of the common peonies I know exhale a modest, powdery softness, or a rosy suggestion.

Imbued with their heritage, I was delighted to find peony bushes growing in the yard of our first military quarters in the early years of our marriage. I brought arms full for bouquets into our sparsely furnished rooms, only to discover emerging blooms covered in ants. After spoiling their gentle breath with insecticide, I learned that dipping the blossoms in warm water was a preferred approach to pest control.

Years later, when my husband and I moved to the South, with its own florid, fragrant delights which cannot survive further north, I still longed for memory-infused peonies. When I spotted a single thriving plant in a lawn near my church, hope revived. My resultant advertisement for peony roots in a farmers' bulletin elicited only one call.

"My dear," began the lyrical Southern voice, "Don't you know you can't grow peonies here? Our winters don't get near cold enough. Where on earth are you from?" When I mentioned my Kansas upbringing and my fond peony memories, the caller launched into an account of her only visit to the state many years earlier by biplane and mule. How could I argue with the voice of such experience, particularly when every gardening resource I consulted gave the same advice to abandon my peony growing ambitions in the South? One catalog responded to my attempted peony order with the following notice: "Our research indicates that this plant is not suited to your climate. We are happy to ship it to you anyway but must inform you that it is not covered by our guarantee."

At last I reconciled myself to the pleasures of growing Southern specialties. But perhaps, I thought, I could convince my mother to dry some of her blossoms for a lasting bouquet. Such efforts ensued. She strung a line in the dark of her basement, carefully selected perfect blossoms, hung them upside down for weeks, and waited. When I visited, she tenderly bundled the precious cargo to carry with me on my return flight. How proudly I arranged my jewel-colored treasures in a favorite green glass vase and described its meaningful history to admiring friends.

One day, I noticed dusty debris beneath the dining room arrangement. When I opened the door of the china cabinet, tiny moths emerged. I found more in the bottom of crystal glasses, others clinging to draperies. Closely examining my valued bouquet,

I found the breeding ground for the room's infestation, tiny larvae which were hatching into moths. Out went my mother's labor of love; in came fumigation.

The silk peonies in my lavabo may not have authentic legacy, but contented me with rich memories of the beloved plant . . . until a green-thumbed friend asked me to identify the strange-leafed plant he had inadvertently scooped with some fragrant jonquils from a grading site. While I stood dumb in astonishment, my husband exploded: "Peony!"

Its single-petal flower with its frilly center was not one of the spectacularly lush varieties which make me swoon, but appeared to be a hardy one. After watching it bloom, our friend gave us the plant. Wistfully, I stuck the peony into the ground; predictably, it died in the heat; resignedly, I assumed it was gone. Imagine my delight and amazement when it reappeared the following spring. Against all the advice of nursery professionals, this gift residing in our garden produced tantalizing buds two recent springs, holding hope in a clench of unopened petals.

On Easter morning this year, my husband beamed, "Have you seen the peony?" Out we raced together. Bright pink rays beamed from its open, blooming face, a smiling tuft inside. Reminding us of the open grave, God once again revealed His affirmation of life.

Ecclesiastes 1:4 says, "Generations come and generations go, but the earth remains forever." Peonies provide the promise of continuity and comforting evidence of God's enduring providence.

Comforting Memory

*F*ragrance can be infused with nostalgia. French author Gustave Flaubert kept his lover's slippers and mittens in his drawer, where their personal scent whispered thoughts of her. In Margaret Mitchell's *Gone with the Wind*, Scarlett remembers the hint of lemon verbena in her mother's fluttering skirts. My perfume consultant describes how the scent of roses always evokes a vivid recollection of her grandmother's footprints in rose-scented dusting powder.

For others, the catalyst for reminiscence may be the odor of pine trees, a hay barn, the sea, sawdust, a dusty country road, ripening grain, canning tomatoes, rain-soaked earth, a kerosene lamp, a doctor's office, moth balls, a chlorinated pool, a shoe store. Each of us retains personal olfactory triggers which conjure reverie. The link between scent and memory might be explained biologically, as our sense of smell connects directly with the limbic system, where emotion and memory reside in the brain. Regardless of rational reason, fragrance has the poignant ability to bear us back in time by reviving memory of a distant person, scene, or emotion.

Memory is why we love and how we survive. Memory keeps significance alive. The slightest whiff of scent remembered can summon an ardent moment with the absent, like a sigh. Marcel Proust writes in *Remembrance of Things Past*, "But when from a long-distant past nothing subsists, after the people are dead . . . taste and smell alone . . . remain poised a long time, like souls, remembering, waiting, hoping, amid the ruins of all the rest, and bear unflinchingly . . . the vast structure of recollection."

The elderly woman with whom I lived during my student teaching always donned her late husband's overcoat to shovel walks after a snowfall. I often wondered whether it was the weight of the wool or her husband's lingering scent which warmed her most. When a loved one is no longer near, sweet reflections on hours together and experiences shared often console us. It is comforting to recall a distant or departed dear one in resonant memories summoned by scent. "Praise be to the God and Father of our Lord Jesus Christ, the Father of compassion and the God of all comfort" (II Corinthians 1:3).

Solitary Refreshment

Consider words that describe a busy and involved individual: sociable, gregarious, companionable, convivial, friendly, genial, affable. Now consider adjectives for someone who enjoys his or her own company: withdrawn, isolated, secluded, forlorn, insular, cloistered, remote, reserved, asocial. Few descriptors would suggest negative connotations for people who like being occupied with the company of others, or positive connotations for those who prefer to be by themselves.

Aspersions are often cast upon those who enjoy solitude, who are not by nature joiners, who dislike crowds, who are disturbed by unsolicited intrusion, who recoil from instant intimacies. Perhaps it is my upbringing which inclines me to appreciate these very qualities of aloneness. Challenges to survival made pioneers a taciturn and self-sufficient lot, reluctant to complain or discuss, had there been someone to listen. Although ameliorated by time and mobility, a vestigial heritage of reticence can yet be noted in rural Midwesterners, comfortable with stillness. While a certain amount of interaction with others is certainly worthy, I believe solitude deserves greater value than it is commonly ascribed.

Diversions to our attentions, time-consuming distractions, unnecessary information, and tedious entertainment creep, increasingly uninvited, into our lives and steal our private moments. We are regularly assaulted by more stimuli than we could possibly process.

Some interaction is, of course, necessary. Co-workers require our cooperation, friendships deserve our attention, and loved ones need our affection, but we might evaluate just how much company is advantageous. Shakespeare admonishes, "Let there be space in your togetherness." Do we need to be plugged into the world and what is happening beyond us from morning until night? How many of the pastimes in which we engage are truly satisfying? Would we really rather be home reading a book? Why aren't we? Are we concerned about how we will be perceived? about what we will miss? Why does it matter? Are we fearful of being alone because we fail to distinguish between singularity and loneliness? Has our interior life so atrophied that we can no longer appreciate intellectual reflection?

One of the greatest delights to be savored in a perfumed garden is the sigh of solitude, a tranquil, healing antidote when the world is too much with us. Regardless where we find escape, the rewards of time alone with our thoughts can restorative. We find the space to revisit old interests, pursue new ones, ponder who we are, muse about our views and beliefs. These placid pleasures which give meaning to our lives cannot occur in the midst of tumult. Romans 14:19 advises, "Let us therefore make every effort to do what leads to peace." We need generous private time to explore the rich interior satisfactions of our own company, to find a serene sufficiency, and to seek the spiritual refreshment described in Psalm 23:2-3: "He leads me beside quiet waters, he restores my soul."

Quiet Please

*W*hat a relief is the open window weather of spring and fall, when breezes once again bear the outdoor smells of earth and plants, the soothing sounds of birds and crickets, and an invitation to join them. Yet even moments out-of-doors are often interrupted by neighbors' barking dogs and the constancy of nearby traffic.

With the first clattering of automobiles on cobblestone, the muffled beating of horse hooves on dirt roads would soon become a memory, and clamor would begin to permeate our world. Tapping telegraph keys diminished distance and compressed time, transforming the remote into the essential. Advancements in industry, communications, transportation, electronics would all take their toll on our quietude.

From the moment we rise in the morning at the babble of the radio alarm, our ears are assaulted with inescapable noise. Television blares with an incessant drone of inane programming and consumer messages. Dishwashers, washing machines, vacuums, and blow dryers roar with the racket of efficiency. Even our refrigerators, computers, furnaces, and air conditioners contribute a persistent background hum.

It is virtually impossible to enter a shop, business, restaurant, or doctor's office without being subjected to someone else's choice of music. Many medical waiting rooms now force patients to listen to pre-selected television programming as well. As these visits are often nerve-wracking enough, such unsolicited sound can be disconcerting.

Electronics seem to have exacerbated the problem. Formerly quiet interludes in public spaces are often now bombarded by an irritating Walkman or clicking laptop. In a check-out line recently, I plainly heard the cell phone user behind me describe to his physician's office, in loud and intimate detail, the symptoms of his current personal malady. In restaurants, I have witnessed cell phone chatter which rudely ignored members of the dining group and interrupted their own attempts at conversation. And much of this egocentric electronic jabber which invades the space and tranquility of others sounds suspiciously like drivel. Couldn't such inconsequential exchange wait for a private moment, or at least until one is out from behind the wheel of a moving vehicle? Screeching tires avoiding an oblivious, yacking driver may be one of the most alarming sounds of all.

Christ tells us in Revelation 3: 20, "Behold I stand at the door and knock: if any man hear my voice, and open the door, I will come in to him." How will we hear His knock in the world's discordant crescendo? We might begin by reducing the volume of surrounding sound. Simple measures might tone down the tumult. Could we reserve electronic devices for truly necessary work? Consider the effects of the noise we generate on others? Read a meditation or say a prayer while stirring the oatmeal instead of instinctively clicking on the morning blather of radio personalities. Opt more often to be entertained by an evening of reading than by television's dissonant decibels? In the newfound hush, we may find our own voices grow softer, learn the rewards of contemplation, rediscover family laughter, and in the exquisite silence, hear God's voice: "Be still and know that I am God" (Psalm 46:10).

Savoring Sassafras

"Ointment and perfume rejoice the heart: so doth the sweetness of a man's friend by hearty counsel"
(Proverbs 27:9 KJV).

Arms full, he stood on our porch in clay-covered work boots and sun-bleached jeans, his red-whiskered chin proudly lifted. Under the bill of his cap, weather-creased eyes expressed the great value of his gift. "This will cure you," he promised.

How dear of our newfound friend, I thought, to offer not only concern, but relief for my ailing back. But while I appreciated his consideration, I could not imagine a therapeutic use for an armload of sticks, unless perhaps they were to prop me up. I peered quizzically at his bundle.

"Found these on a grading job. Smelled it before we even saw it," he continued. Still, I must have looked puzzled. "I dug 'em up for you." I began to thumb through my mental inventory of limited entries on the subject of roots. "They're hard to find, and tough to dig, but it's a nice bunch," he said.

Such exuberant sincerity, and I couldn't even identify his offering. My ignorance became obvious.

"Sassafras!" he exploded, extending the sandy roots.

The gift, revealed, pleased me immediately. It delighted my herbalist tendencies and our newcomers' interest in natural and cultural curiosities of the South. Slow and bent, I bore the roots into the kitchen as proudly as my back permitted.

My only knowledge of sassafras came from novels about the Old South, in which country folks drank sassafras tea on summer porches. (I could not recall its being sipped on fine verandahs.) The tea's medicinal properties were exactly what our friend had in mind. I inquired how to make the curative concoction.

"Just cut it up and pour water over it, I reckon," the outdoorsman advised as he left the kitchen's constraints.

My husband and I examined the woody jumble, washed them, and determined we needed a saw to reduce the tough, unwieldy roots to manageable size. Off my husband went to borrow one from our neighbor. He returned with more discoveries—the easy willingness of next-door lending, a handsaw which looked as if it might fell a small sapling, and a treasured regional cookbook containing a recipe for sassafras tea. The last rendered the hand-saw unnecessary. It is the bark, we learned, which is used for tea.

Stripping the root's bark revealed its fragrant, rosy lining. Ah, here was the essence for which the tea is enjoyed. For me it recalled frothy mugs of A&W root beer in our family station wagon and its holes in the floorboard. I began to understand how this aroma arouses nostalgia.

Eager to sample the elixir, touted by the old recipe as spring tonic, I brewed and tasted the hot tea. Next I tried a stronger brew over ice. That was it! Enthused by success, we delivered a full Mason jar to our lending neighbor. What pleasure it gave us to sit on his front porch and introduce a real Southerner to a taste of his own culture. But, while the tea had quenched our neighbor's thirst, it had only whet mine to know more about this fascinating sassafras.

Sassafras, I learned, is a tall native North American tree of the laurel family. It thrives along the Eastern coast, and it is said that its strong aroma alerted Columbus that he was approaching land. Spanish explorers were first to catalog its medicinal properties, along with those of other healing herbs used by aboriginal Americans. Eventually, sassafras became one of America's earliest commercial exports to Europe, where it was used in soap and shampoo.

Oil extracted from bark of the root was a popular ingredient of "cure-all" tonics, mouthwashes and medicines, including a drug used to treat syphilis. Sassafras was purported to have at once stimulating and relaxing properties. Its power to increase perspiration earned its reputation for reducing fevers. So, I found the reason sassafras refreshes on a hot day.

The history of sassafras if full of other curious applications. Because its wood dries with less shrinkage than other hardwood, it was often used for fences and for boaters' prized "sassie" paddles. The vermin-controlling reputation of its odor prompted use of sassafras wood in constructing bedsteads, slave-cabin floors, and hen-roosts.

Sassafras leaves appear on the same tree in three different shapes—three-lobed, mitten, and oval. These aromatic leaves ground into powder are known as filé, a thickening agent used in Cajun and Creole gumbos. Another mystery was solved. None of our new Southern acquaintances seemed to know just what was meant by the term in the familiar song lyric, "jambalaya, crawfish pie, filé gumbo." Now we all know.

While I regret that I found a herniated disc beyond its curative powers, sassafras has been a boon to us in other ways. Its curiosities have been a means of connecting with the South and with its people. Sassafras was only the first of many gifts our friend has offered us. From him we have learned about Southern manner and mindset. We've explored memories in old neighborhoods. We've heard about haints and stood midst swarms of feeding hummingbirds. We've embraced the esteem of kin. We've sampled collards and crowder peas. We've experienced bass-voiced pond frogs and surface-slapping catfish on a still night.

In our process of exploration, just beneath the bark of Southern roots, we've discovered an especially savory gift of sassafras—the fragrant pleasure of friendship.

Should you wish to sample a little sassafras, or to share some with a friend, here is my recipe for Sassafras Tea: Steep a generous amount of the dried root bark (available in health food stores) in hot water until tea reaches desired strength. Strain into a clean pitcher. Dilute if necessary. Chill. Serve over ice. Sweeten if desired.

Please note that sassafras bark does contain a carcinogen called safrole, which can be avoided by using filtered sassafras concentrate found in grocery stores.

(This essay originally appeared in the Spring 1995 issue of *Georgia Journal* and was subsequently revised.)

Elusive Allure

*A*s I strolled across the campus courtyard, I was overwhelmed by a provocative profusion of scent. The effluence seemed to envelope me, then hide, then reappear, teasing, taunting, tantalizing. What was the source of this enticing, alluring, elusive aura? Glancing about the grounds, I saw no blooming shrubbery or blossoming flowers. Perhaps I had imagined it. But then, on a breeze, the intriguing redolence arrived again. In the leafy arbor of the cherry laurel which branched above me, I discovered tiny blossoms fragrantly flirting with me.

The source of scent in the garden is often elusive. One moment it can waft rhapsodic, and the next, all traces have vanished. Happiness often evades us in much the same manner. Almost within our grasp, the object of our desire recedes. The more desperately we attempt to attain it, the more remote it seems. Advertising today promises we can achieve happiness with our next purchase, but when the illusions fail us, we are left feeling dissatisfied, needy, unfulfilled, depressed. Even the temporary pleasures of prosperity, attention, and achievement cannot fill the void in us, the yearning for lasting satisfaction. In the words of Alexis de Tocqueville, "The incomplete joys of this world will never satisfy [the] heart." Temporary gratification, although compelling, is illusory.

How, then, can we find the source of true and enduring happiness? Such fulfillment can billow from above. Jesus advises, "Seek first his kingdom and his righteousness, and all these things will be given to you as well" (Matthew 6:33). The balm and blessing of God's over-branching boughs can imbue our lives with the sweet contentment of His pervading goodness.

Looking Up

*S*tudents sloshed in with squeaking shoes, the smell of wet jackets, and bumping umbrellas, which puddled on the floor. Those of us leaving passed the jumble of dripping arrivals in the dimly lit classroom corridor and emerged into the dreary shade of a low-limbed tree. Umbrellas popped, a fine drizzle squelched conversation and muffled sound, the morning as still and uninspired as students had been in class. We dodged passing students sharing the narrow, uneven brick walkway, watching our feet, avoiding puddles, careful not to stumble, or slip, or step in a muddy rut.

Our vision and thoughts seemingly asleep, a bright flash appeared ahead. I stopped abruptly, an audible exclamation escaping. The few students who could not skirt the traffic obstruction followed my glance to find what had prompted their instructor's present episode of derangement. Swarms of yellow slickers, the campus grounds crew, were transplanting brilliant, blazing, yellow lilies on this darkest of Monday mornings—a spot of busy sunshine. Soon the vivid patch would drench us with fragrant delight.

I doubt that on a sunny day we would have found the scene so remarkable or mood changing, but now the simple bright moment jolted those of us who saw it to life. All we had to do was shift our sight from the potential difficulties beneath our feet, and look up.

What blessings are we missing because we are mired in the mud of worry, silenced by self-interest, depressed by inconsequential concerns? A new vision can be a simple matter of changing our sights. Colossians 3:2 recommends, "Set you minds on things above, not on earthly things." What are we spending our time and thoughts dwelling on? Are they positive, uplifting? If not, we might send up a prayer and raise our eyes with the psalmist, who resolves, "In the morning will I direct my prayers unto thee, and will look up" (Psalm 5:3 KJV).

Blessings Preserved

*M*y mother's late summer kitchen was suffused with the savor of seasonal canning and a sharp current of vinegar. Hot jars lining countertops sealed with satisfying plinks. At the height of harvest, large kettles were hardly put away before the next vegetables were picked and ready. Mother could regularly be found with a large pan of beans in her lap, tediously snapping and stringing. Then came the day-long process of washing, filling jars, twisting lids, and boiling kettles. On occasion, we lent a hand skinning and cutting tomatoes, the stinging, acidic juice running down our arms. Then there were plums, peaches, and cherries to pit, and cucumbers to slice for bread and butter pickles.

By summer's end, colorful jars filled shelves with fruits and vegetables preserved for winter's pleasure. In times when fresh produce was not readily available out of season, it always seemed a kind of miracle to be able to enjoy the taste of sunny days when gardens slept in snow.

The process of preserving inhibits harmful bacteria from spoiling our harvest much like God preserves us from personal afflictions which seek to destroy us. Our heart, body, and spirit are all preyed upon. Relationships suffer, health betrays, the world entices. It seems impossible to know rationally why God allows such affliction. We can no more understand the misery we must endure than we can fathom the richness of God's defense and protection. His almighty presence sustains us in our trials and strengthens us to meet the challenges which confront us. "Remember your word to your servant, for you have given me hope. My comfort in my suffering is this: Your promise preserves my life" (Psalm 119:49-50). God promises to preserve us from peril and provide in us the fruit of His blessing.

Evanescent Season

W inds rise, temperatures drop, and in the words of Emily
Dickinson, "the morns are meeker than they were."
Autumn breezes in. Sweaters tumble out. John Keats
calls these late months the "Season of mists and mellow fruitfulness,/
Close bosom-friend of the maturing sun." Hovering mists capture the
smells of fall fecundity and decaying debris. Shadows lengthen.
Days shorten. Light arrives late, yawns, and leaves early. Remnant
days of the calendar slowly expire.

In seasonal images, the Bible causes us to contemplate the brevity of
our remaining days. "What is your life?" asks James 4:14 and
answers its own question: "You are a mist that appears for a little
while and then vanishes."

If fall were the permanent end of natural life, or if the Fall in Eden
were the permanent end of spiritual life, we would be doomed indeed.
But the words of I Peter 1:3-4 reassure us that when summer's bright
bouquets have breathed their last, and our days of maturing and
decline commit us to earth, a season of new vitality will follow:
"Praise be to the God and Father of our Lord Jesus Christ! In his
great mercy he has given us new birth into a living hope through the
resurrection of Jesus Christ from the dead, and into an inheritance that
can never perish, spoil, or fade—kept in heaven for you."

The church calendar parallels our seasons here. As autumn closes, we
consider sin's deadly effect. While roots develop their strength
underground in the bleak of winter, we celebrate the Savior's birth.
When plants spring to life, we rise with His resurrection promise. Brief
though our seasons be on earth, in the company of our "close bosom-
friend," God's Son, our days will stretch ahead, vital and eternal.

Redolent Root Cellar

s a youngster, I entered into the dim depths of my grandfather's root cellar hesitantly, behind my mother's skirts, until I grew more brazen with age. But the retreat from light into its darkness gave me a sense of how the mythological goddess Persephone must have felt when she descended annually to the underworld. As my toes searched their way down slippery stone stairs to a cool moistness, my face felt a faint, unwelcome, indistinguishable sensation—a cobweb whose size and position I could not quite detect. I flailed to brush it aside, wondering just where that spider may currently be residing . . . and how big it was. A rich, dank aroma infused my damp descent. At the bottom of the stairs, I retrieved knobby, soil-encrusted potatoes from the bins, catching a pungent rotting whiff from one corner.

It wasn't the temperature which sent a chill up my spine so much as the sensation that I was becoming part of the earth, permeated and suffused by its rank mustiness. How much dirt might be between me and the sky? I wouldn't say the experience was entirely unpleasant, but rather, enticing in its strange other-worldliness. Suddenly startled by a hopping toad, I scampered toward the bright afternoon above.

Despite its chilling atmosphere, I had to admire the cellar's tough, persistent life. My grandfather's root cellar remains frightfully appealing to me in the mysterious paradox of how those edibles dug from the earth could then be returned underground, kept from rotting, and retrieved to sustain a family through a long Midwestern winter . . . until it was once again time to plant and harvest a new season's crop. What a vivid image of God's power to sustain, renew, and resurrect!

Dreams of Heaven

The Bible gives us no precise picture of heaven. Many of the images which describe Paradise are painted in opulent metaphor to convey its splendor in human terms that we may comprehend. When I read about jeweled streets, I imagine the gemlike colors of beautifully fragrant blossoms—of diamond jasmine, emerald herbs, gold honeysuckle, ruby roses, and pearl gardenias. My personal vision of heaven is one of the first garden in all its perfection, before it was spoiled by sin. If God created such a sublime natural world for our original home, I like to think that He may restore us to live in that garden as His divine plan intended.

When I contemplate our world's breathtaking evidence of the hereafter—sweet summer's grassy lap, verdant glades, still water ablaze with sunset, the longing coo of dove—how can I imagine a realm more heavenly than this?

Human limitations make it is difficult to conceive of the life that awaits us in the company of our Lord. Regardless of how we picture heaven now, we know that it will exceed all our expectations. "We are looking forward to a new heaven and a new earth, the home of righteousness" (II Peter 3:13). For those who believe in God's promise of salvation, it will be a dream come true.

Revising Creation

While living and traveling in Europe, we relished the abundance of fresh flower markets. Drifts of bright delectables from farm gardens filled cobblestone plazas. My husband bought me lilies of the valley from the gnarled hands of a weathered gardener in her flowered kerchief and frayed sweater, who offered them tenderly as the treasure they were. Inexpensive, fragrant flowers regularly graced our quarters.

For scented bouquets, I now rely on bundles of our herbs, snippings from flowering shrubs, and garden cuttings. On occasions when I have sought a special bouquet from the florist, I have often been disappointed by the scentless selections available. Even carnations, roses, and other varieties long recognized for their fragrance seem often to be missing their perfumed appeal. Hybridized and cultivated for transport and longevity, many of the flowers I commonly encounter for sale have been deprived of one of their most appealing qualities. Happily, some flower breeders have begun to recognize this loss and are once again making old-fashioned scented varieties available to gardeners. I hope to see evidence that scent will become more widely valued in florist offerings as well.

This trend of manipulating nature for specific qualities concerns me. I am uneasy about human beings selecting properties which we deem, in our limited wisdom, to be most advantageous. I worry that we are unable to envision distant implications or understand the elaborate interrelationships of which the pieces we alter are only a part. Changing what appear to be minor elements, even when alterations seem improvements, may have repercussions we cannot now imagine until damage has been irrevocably done.

When we begin to modify forms of life, whose standards will be applied, and whose welfare will be considered in choosing attributes? In the case of flowers bred for marketing, preferences other than scent have taken precedence. How will questions of conflicting interests in more consequential circumstances be resolved? Whose will should prevail?

Ecclesiastes 3:14 declares, "Everything God does will endure forever; nothing can be added to it and nothing taken from it. God does it so that men will revere him." These words should give us pause. We cannot begin to comprehend the intricacies of God's infinite wisdom, proclaimed in Romans 11:30: "Oh, the depth of the riches of the wisdom and knowledge of God! How unsearchable his judgments, and his paths beyond tracing out!" We certainly need to proceed with great care to avoid damaging or destroying the delicate balance of His creation by our audacious revision.

Cultivating Taste

lthough we think of taste as being a finely discriminating sense, in actuality, the mouth can detect only salt, sweet, sour, and bitter. It is unlikely that we could distinguish between tea and coffee, for example, if we pinched our noses while drinking the distinct beverages. Consider how we lose our sense of taste when congested with a head cold. Most nuances we describe as taste are actually aromas we sniff and exhale as we drink or chew.

I recall the intensity of tastes and aromas from my grandfather's garden. The crack of watermelon on his summer porch spilled pink perfume. A patch of lacy dill, destined for puckery, home-made pickles, suffused the shade of a soft, still evening. Pungent tomato stalks scented hands reaching for the warm, juicy globes. Now we can buy them all year long—pale, pulpy impostors.

A chilly spring-water swish under the farmyard hydrant revealed the crisp, sweet flesh of slender carrots. In the grocery store recently, from his perch in his mother's shopping cart, a youngster eyed me closely as I selected a fresh bunch of fern-topped carrots. "Oh, Mommy!" he squealed, "Let's get some bunny rabbit carrots!" I understood why the vegetable in its original foliage seemed such a novelty to him when his mother placed plastic-bagged carrots in her basket, ignoring his plea.

Strawberries were named in Latin, *fraga*, for their remarkable fragrance. I remember the velvet sweetness of those my grandfather grew. Under the shady leaves of his well-tended plants hid small, crimson fruits, their tender pulp ambrosial. Our dessert bowls never seemed to hold enough of the delicacies. Contrast this pleasure with that of supermarket varieties today. Cultivated for transport and appearance, they are big, bright, hard, and tasteless, although they will last days in the refrigerator. The beautiful Indian name for strawberry is heart-berry. Sadly, today's mass-produced berry seems to have lost its heart.

We can find nearly any kind of produce year round in most supermarket produce departments, but spongy out-of-season tomatoes or plums are not worth the bother of bringing home. A single, sublime bowl of strawberries in season, warm from the garden, farmer's market, road-side stand, or pick-your-own patch, with a drizzle of cream and honey may be preferable to regular helpings on demand. Punctuating the year with such sensory moments connects us with nature's distinct intervals and with the earth just now beneath our feet. We value the here and now. Eating seasonally not only offers incomparable flavor and greater nutritional benefit, but also encourages local farmers to continue to make their produce available.

At the conclusion of the Civil War, over eight hundred varieties of apples were available from American nurseries. Today, of the thirty or so apple varieties available from commercial nurseries, only about ten are commonly sold. These are the easiest to grow, least perishable, and most economic to market. Because taste is often rendered insignificant in the editing process of mass commercial production, it is worth seeking out private orchards which may still offer rare tree-ripened treasures.

Our eating has become debased. We settle for trifling satisfactions, as long as they are quick and easy. Despite the relentless influx of novelty everywhere confronting us, our palates seem terribly apathetic. When we buy food for convenience, taste and smell lose priority. Consumers who do not know the succulence of personally grown produce will not seek it. But by relinquishing our involvement in choices so vital and pleasurable as food, we become impoverished.

"Oh taste and see that the Lord is good," says Psalm 34:8. In the fruits of the earth, we enjoy evidence of God's delicious providence. American supermarkets offer some of the greatest abundance in the world. Yet, how unrecognizable many of these grocery products must appear to the Creator today.

Spirited Flavor

*H*ave you ever taken an apple in your pocket on a fresh, fall ramble? Pausing on a lichened log after an invigorating walk intensifies the pleasure of the fruit. Consider other experiences eating out of doors. How much better a toasty hot dog over a country bonfire tastes and smells than the boiled, pallid stove-top counterpart. Contrast the aroma of hamburger on the backyard grill to the greasy stink when fried in the kitchen. Or compare the flavor of the same lunch eaten in a park or at an office desk. Fresh air and exercise not only benefit our health, but also enliven our senses. Our tastes are understandably depressed when we spend the majority of our days in the closed atmosphere of our homes, cars, and workplaces. A picnic seems to perk up the palate.

In a spiritual sense, when we are imbued with God's wholesome breath and we exercise His will, we increase our appetite for goodness. Galatians 5:22-23, 25 describes the qualities for which we acquire a taste. "The fruit of the Spirit is love, joy, peace, longsuffering, gentleness, goodness, faith, meekness, temperance . . . If we live in the Spirit, let us also walk in the Spirit" (KJV).

The world does not always appreciate these fruits. Such seasoned qualities can seem impalatable to those in the marketplace. Suppressing personal desires to the needs of others, answering softly when angered, accepting hardship can taste unappetizing in the mouth of the spiritually deprived. And our own Spirited taste can diminish when we live bound by the preferences of the marketplace. As we notice that gratifying oneself, speaking one's mind, and complaining are practiced and valued by those around us, we are inclined to develop a taste for such behavior. We need to seek the Spirit's bracing wind with walks in scripture, church, and prayer to restore our ability to savor and share the zesty flavor of His fruit.

Natural Odors

*A*s children, we had the great advantage of regular visits to my grandfather's farm where strong smells were an integral part of nature and its husbandry— steaming silage, slippery manure, the acrid chicken coop, an oily machine shop. One of the most odiferous events was butchering chickens. My uncles beheaded them with a mighty, cracking whack of the ax. When headless bodies quit flailing, my mother and aunts scalded the birds in a great steaming tub, the air reeking of wet hens. They littered the ground with plucked feathers, singed the stinking birds (and often arm hairs) over an old wood-burning stove in the wash house, then tediously removed pinfeathers. At the kitchen sink, the women plunged their hands inside still warm birds, extracting slippery globs of innards. Smelly buckets of entrails buzzed with flies in the summer heat. Washed and cut into pieces, the chickens were finally wrapped in paper for freezing. From such repulsive processing came the enticing aroma of golden fried chicken.

In our modern world, we are distant from nature as a sustaining force in our lives. We buy our chickens ready to cook, neatly packaged in plastic, without raising, butchering, and dressing them ourselves. We get water instantly from a convenient tap, instead of worrying if the well is clear enough or full enough for our needs. If temperatures are too warm or too cool, we simply switch our indoor thermostat to a comfortable setting. And what blessings these advancements are—as those who remember days without them will surely agree.

But today in our air-conditioned, sanitized, convenient world, we may not as clearly recognize God's generosity nor our responsibility to maintain the bounty He provides. Our modern civilization is distant from the cycles of the seasons, impervious to weather, disconnected from the land and its creatures, and unaccustomed to the natural. While we are not inclined give up the comforts we have come to enjoy, perhaps we would benefit from an awareness of and a closeness to nature, which many of us experience today only through the sealed windows of airless buildings.

Earlier generations were more intimately acquainted with the precious nature of God's gifts in His natural world. My parents remember plentiful wild berries—raspberries, blackberries, gooseberries, grapes—which are rarely found today. Widespread use of agricultural pesticides has destroyed them almost completely in only a few short decades. A younger generation cannot regret their loss because they do not remember them.

Even products we consider healthy, less processed, or labeled organic are rarely altogether "natural," and most of the food we consume has not been for centuries. Recently, I spotted a new message on the label of an "all fruit" jam I have long enjoyed in an effort to avoid refined sugars: "NOW GMO FREE." "What harmful ingredient had the product previously contained?" I wondered. The fine print indicated the spread no longer contains genetically modified organisms. I had never thought to be concerned about this prospect.

How aware are we of the conditions under which animals and produce we consume today are raised and processed? How informed are we about the effects of what we consume on our health, including processing, additives, and genetic manipulation designed to make products look, smell, and taste appealing in their long transit to consumers? What do we know about the purity of our natural resources? How conscious are we of the effects of our wanton use on their levels? And what are we doing about any of these matters?

An analogy might be drawn between our indiscriminate choices of entertainment and food. Just as our culture becomes decreasingly able to entertain itself and settles for the paltry pabulum pre-selected by an entertainment industry, so we become passive consumers of products which the food industry has persuaded us to prefer. Eaters who lose interest in how food is produced tend to abandon responsibility for the resources on which nourishment depends.

Being informed about what we eat inspires us to respect and care for the land and all that depends upon it. An awareness of our responsible place in God's world is essential to promoting healthy habits and attitudes. David's praise in Psalm 24:1 reminds us, "The earth is the Lord's and everything in it, the world, and all who live in it." Only when we appreciate God's largess to us can we be careful stewards of His natural provisions and attentive caretakers of our physical well-being.

Living Water

offered my usual request. "Water, please." Our friend in rural Indiana took us to a widening in the road for fuel, supplies, and lunch at a clattering cafe filled with flannel shirts, overalls, and caps advertising fertilizer and feed. Raising the plastic glass to my lips, I noted an odd smell. One sip identified the taste—gasoline. I glanced around the room to see if anyone else was drinking this obvious toxin. There appeared to be few water glasses on the Formica tables, but I had to wonder about the taste of the iced tea and coffee being swilled. A next-door service station seemed the likely culprit in fouling the well water. Did no one care, or had regulars become gradually inured to the taste?

I confess. I am a water drinker. I firmly believe in the healthful properties of keeping the body well hydrated. Because I consume so much water, moving to a new community always requires some adjustment to the smell and taste of the tap's varying amounts of minerals and chlorine. When I lived in a small town in Missouri, I found the smell and taste of tap water oddly "off." My stainless steel cutlery left in a damp sink rusted overnight. Frightened by what internal corrosion the water may be wreaking, I phoned the municipal water utility for information about local water. A week later, a large manila envelope arrived, filled with water test results—page after page of chemical analysis only a scientist might interpret. I didn't begin to know how to translate these reams of information in answer to my simple question: Was my water safe to drink?

I began to investigate home water treatment options. But what did they remove? Minerals? microbes? chlorine? And weren't some of these elements good for one? How much was too much? Then there was the matter of installation—under the sink, on the faucet, in a pitcher? And cost was no small item for equipment, installation, maintenance, filters. How was one to make sense of it all? I threw up my hands and endured the taste and threat from the tap.

Still I wonder about the sources of our water. How do we know how pure it is? What is dumped upstream before it reaches us? How effective are purification measures? My concerns have not become paranoia; I still drink water directly from the tap, recognizing that the sources of even bottled water can be questionable. Reports that American water supplies are some of the cleanest in the world assure me . . . somewhat.

Because Europe's history of clean water sources had not always been dependable, we found while living there that most natives chose beer, wine, or an occasional ice-less soft drink. How was a committed water drinker to survive? Our initial requests for bottled water resulted in sprightly carbonated versions. We tried still water, which also contained a degree of fizz. Finally, a German friend gave us the appropriate term—Leitungswasser—which literally translates "from the pipe." This request, however, was usually met with raised eyebrows and an incredulous query to confirm that we did indeed intend to drink water which was generally reserved for cooking, washing, and bathing.

In France, drinking water was easier to acquire. There we needed not resort to the suspicious tap; bottled spring water was everywhere available.

While vacationing in Gran Canaria, we were cautioned, as in many countries where water is suspect, against drinking the water or anything with ice, or eating uncooked fruits and vegetables that may have been washed in it. Despite our care, I found myself racing from the breakfast table the first few mornings of our visit.

Thirst quenching water was a distinct quest for the ancient desert traveler. While traveling through Samaria, Jesus asked for a drink from a woman who came to draw well water. He used the occasion to tell her about the promise of living water: "Everyone who drinks this water will be thirsty again, but whoever drinks the water I give him will never thirst. Indeed, the water I give him will become in him a spring of water welling up to eternal life" (John 4:13). The

Samaritan woman did not completely comprehend His allusions to such a life-giving force, until Jesus identified Himself as the promised Savior. Just as our bodies need clean drinking water for health and survival, so we require the water of the Spirit—to purify, revive, and sustain our souls.

Creation Conscious

$\mathcal{S}$tanding in the middle of a Kansas prairie, where the scent of grass and sage rise in the heat of the sun and waft on relentless wind, where heavens touch horizons in every direction, we might easily feel that our earth and its resources are boundless. I recall my reacquaintance with this sense of space after the close congestion of European living, the heady affinity with the natural world at the end of outstretched fingertips. The grand expanse and endless vistas of these landscapes drew settlement westward. A vast, untamed wilderness appeared to offer possibility, promise, and plenty for everyone.

Before long, a heedless profligacy was unleashed. Buffalo were killed with such abandon that their numbers hovered near extinction for many years. Enormous heaps of buffalo bones dotted the plains, piled near newly built railroads for shipment to Eastern factories, where they were made into fine bone china teacups. To satisfy demand for beef, grasslands were often overgrazed, doing irreparable damage to prairie ecosystems.

The mirage of infinite space has vanished, and now there are hordes of us occupying most inhabited areas, crowding the land and each other. Rash and ravenous, we squander, spoil, and shrink our breathing room. Nature's buoyant resilience is sorely tested. Our burning of fossil fuels stinks our air and depletes oxygen, noise deafens us, asphalt devours green life, effluence defiles our water, wanton waste sickens our souls. Ongoing conflicts between nature and technology are not easy to reconcile. In the course of our country's history, technology has enabled us to transform the barren into the bountiful. But our drive to control and enhance nature has also taken a toll on the essential land, air, and water which sustain us.

Seemingly unlimited resources have lulled us into careless and destructive use of them in pursuit of greater goods and comforts, encouraged by prosperity, media hype, and the psychology of self-esteem. "I'm worth it!" too often translates into "I will deny myself nothing, regardless of expense to the world or others with whom I share it." Prudence, thrift, and self-denial seem to have disappeared from the dictionary of self-gratification. When our society promotes the prodigal expenditure of time, energies, finances, and other resources, why should nature be exempt?

Why does the public recoil from conservation? Do we lack information, reason, restraint, responsibility, resolve? The stealthy degradation of nature and its effect on our well-being appears to have little effect on our consciousness. When we view nature only in terms of its benefit to ourselves, we soon lose sight of its value. So what can be done to promote preservation of our environment?

First we must recognize that this sphere on which we reside and depend is not inexhaustible, that there are limits to the quantity and purity of our natural resources. Then we must make deliberate, individual commitment to changing our ruthless and impudent abuse of them. To inspire such awareness and action, we will need to become receptive to the ephemeral loveliness of creation, to the spiritual refreshment it offers, and to the vital harmony between man and nature. When God surveyed the world He had made, he judged it "very good" (Genesis 1:31). We also must acknowledge the value of His creation to both our physical and spiritual nourishment, and our personal obligation to preserve this sacred relationship.

Drenched with Power

*H*ow I love the welcome smell of summer showers—
the healthy, loamy breath which rises from the
soaked earth, breezes through the screen door, and
causes me to inhale deeply. Rain, of course, does not always
respire so gently.

Few seasonal spectacles must rival the drama of a prairie storm.
A suggestion of gray on the horizon can quickly mound and swell
into dark, surging billows. The air begins to prickle with the scent
of anticipation, rousing the yawning landscape. Rising currents stir,
then gust, then blow. Pattering drops turn to stinging, horizontal
torrents. Umbrellas pop inside-out, fabric ripped away, useless.
Street throngs dash for cover. At home, windows and doors slam
shut against gales. Thunder rolls and crashes; lightening slices the
firmament.

When skies loom green and air grows still, tornadoes threaten.
Having seen their devastation first hand, our Kansas family took no
chances. Unimpeded on the plains, snapping branches too near,
night winds often chased us into cellars. Flashlights, candles, and
matches in hand, we dashed for shelter, nightgowns and robes
flapping in the gale. As visions of Dorothy and Toto danced in our
heads, we listened to reports of funnel sightings on a transistor
radio and recoiled from water bugs sharing our shelter and seeking
our pajamas.

If ever there were evidence of God's power and glory, these
storms were it. Job 36:26-37:5 gives an awe-inspiring account of
God's power:

How great is God—beyond understanding! . . .

He draws up the drops of water, which distill as rain to the streams;

the clouds pour down their moisture and abundant showers fall on mankind.

Who can understand how he spreads out the clouds, how he thunders from his pavilion?

See how he scatters his lightning about him, bathing the depths of the sea.

This is the way he governs the nations and provides food in abundance.

He fills his hands with lightning and commands it to strike its mark.

His thunder announces the coming storm; even the cattle make known its approach.

At this my heart pounds and leaps from its place.

Listen! Listen to the roar of his voice, to the rumbling that comes from his mouth. He unleashes his lightning beneath the whole heaven and sends it to the ends of the earth.

After that comes the sound of his roar; he thunders with his majestic voice. When his voice resounds, he holds nothing back.

God's voice thunders in marvelous ways; he does great things beyond our understanding.

God drenches us in evidence of His power, saturating our senses with the freshness of impending rain, the reverberation of thunder, the tingling energy of the wind, and the reviving deluge of showers. We are moved to join David in prayer: "Yours, O Lord, is the greatness and the power and the glory and the majesty and the splendor, for everything in heaven and earth is yours. Yours, O Lord, is the kingdom; you are exalted as head over all" (I Chronicles 29:11).

More of Less

*P*ersonal fragrance is not always so personal. Sometimes instead of whispering intimacies to dear ones, perfume announces its arrival to the crowd. An overly strong essence or a too-generous splash can overwhelm those beyond personal boundaries. Offended and allergic readers of some magazines containing unsolicited scent strips have successfully lobbied publishers for their removal.

Too much of a fragrance can impede our ability to distinguish the nuances of neighboring scent. An intense bouquet of lilacs as a dinner party centerpiece or heavily perfumed candles would overwhelm the subtle tastes of food and destroy the pleasure of diners. Perfumers must judiciously blend their elixirs so one note does not overpower another. They strive for a balanced result in which each separate component complements another. When it comes to fragrance, as with so much else in life, excess is seldom advantageous.

While our computer was in the shop for repair, the technician asked whether I might like more RAM or ROM or some such capability added to increase the speed of the sluggish machine. As I considered the cost of the increase, a young employee chimed, "More is better!" The gentleman assisting me turned to challenge the youth's facile observation: "Would more D's on your report card be better?" He had struck directly on a trend I have been observing—an increasing demand for more.

When Mother took us for a rare treat to the local drugstore soda fountain or to Woolworth's for a warm weather drink, the common size of a cherry Coke was eight ounces—one cup. We delighted in every fizzy, fruity sip. Remember the size of the original small strawberry soda bottle pulled through a series of rows and levers from the cold chest of a service station vending machine? Today's convenience store soft drink can be 44 ounces—five and a half cups! The take-home bottle is two liters—almost eight and a half cups. Does the human body now require so much more hydration? Restaurant portions are often so generous we cannot finish them, nor, judging by the size of the overweight population, do we need them.

The average size of new homes continues to increase. How much distance from each other do our smaller families need? Bath towels today are advertised as "over-sized." Such dimensions may feel luxurious, but require more loads, water, and detergents to launder. The sport utility vehicle is today's most popular transportation. Never mind that its off-road capabilities will likely never be needed by the suburban mom running errands and taxiing children. Ignore the fact that its size obstructs vision, crowds parking spaces, requires skilled handling, and compromises natural resources to manufacture and fuel. Our growing expectations come to be considered normal. Standard size becomes large, extra large, super, jumbo, mammoth, colossal, gargantuan. And it is not just size that is increasing, it is quantity as well. We might take a peek in our closets and drawers and calculate the clothes. A new shopping center in my community destroyed acres and acres of air-cleansing trees to build multiple new stores, which, for the most part, duplicate similar products and services already available elsewhere. Each store has rack upon rack of more merchandise each season to fuel consumers' insatiable greed. We work harder to spend more. Increasing headaches require greater medication. Eventually, all our more and bigger stuff ends in more and bigger landfills, excessive detritus.

Conservation is unpopular. So is self-denial. We want more, we want it our way, and we want it now. Recalling the Biblical counsel to be careful stewards of our blessings, we might consider the cost of our acquisitive and consumptive demands to others, to the environment, to space on the planet, to our mental, physical, and spiritual well being. Expediency and personal gratification cannot always coexist compatibly with the greater good. Discriminating choices are needed. Just as our olfactory nerve endings become fatigued and insensitive when saturated with or exposed to a scent for a prolonged time, so we lose our ability to distinguish between surfeit and sufficiency.

Growth is not intrinsically bad. More can be better. More generosity, more compassion, more healthful surroundings, more contemplation would certainly benefit us all. But to gain these, we will have to do with less of so much else.

The admonition of Hebrews 13:5 remains pertinent: "Be content with what you have."

The Treasure of Trees

When my parents lived in the country, I rode my bicycle on rural roads. As I whirred through a small streamside stand of trees, I could smell the cool green foliage and feel temperatures dip perceptively, even on the hottest days. Gold-fish in my grandfather's stock tank caught a glint of sunlight through the rustling leaves of towering cottonwoods. Teachers made of game of picking dandelions in the grassy shadows of schoolyard limbs. On summer afternoons, we made daisy chains or looked for four-leaf clovers under the sweet branches of shade trees in our front lawn.

God planted those trees and made us caretakers of them. "And the Lord God made all kinds of trees grow out of the ground—trees that were pleasing to the eye and good for food" (Genesis 2:9). "The Lord God took the man and put him in the Garden of Eden to work it and take care of it" (Genesis 2:15). Today, however, we often seem to have abandoned our appointment as custodians and lost concern for our charges.

In my own neighborhood, rows of beautiful willow trees were recently wrenched from a stream bed at the presumed threat that tree roots might impede water flow and increase potential for future flooding. Borrowing trouble and raising the specter of "liability" stirred up sufficient financial concern until trees became victim.

In our community is plenty of evidence that nature is readily sacrificed at the altar of economics. It often seems the only valued green is money. Acres of midtown woods have been razed to expand shopping. Yet earlier projects, which denuded expansive areas, now sit vacant. Near our home, more lands filled with ancient trees have been clear cut for business. Replacement efforts are usually feeble—a young sapling or two, decades away from maturity, to appease the "tree-huggers."

I attempt to raise consciousness. Developers respond to my letters with the platitude that not everyone cares for trees. When I point out local environmental damage to students, they ask, oblivious, "What trees?" and express delight in the plethora of new stores and restaurants, which have replaced woods and groves. Aiming for outrage, I can't even rally concern.

Destruction, or course, has long accompanied our country's expansion. Space has felt so boundless that conservation has seemed unnecessary. Our needs are being met and our desires indulged, and we have not yet come face to face with personal repercussions of natural carnage. It is hard to stir concern when the value of trees seems so ephemeral and hard to measure. Providing homes for birds, slowing run-off, reducing air temperatures, absorbing noise, offering shade, cleansing the atmosphere—how can monetary value be placed on these?

We seem intent on offering today's children every economic advantage, but what about their sensory enrichment? Today, when I drive past the treeless playground of a nearby daycare center, I consider how these youngsters' awareness of God's world is diminished, of the pleasures deprived them. I begin to understand how those who have never learned to appreciate nature can so easily dispense with it.

Apple Spill

*I*magine an autumn walk on a seldom-traveled country path. Suddenly a vivid ripeness reaches from beyond a bend. A few steps further reveal an aromatic and unexpected apple fall. The startling red bounty perfuses the lane and prompts a delightful detour. All these pleasures because no one harvested the appealing abundance of apples! Restraint can often yield unexpected benefits like these.

In fact, a failure of restraint in Eden's original garden initiated iniquity. Adam and Eve sought God's perfect knowledge for themselves and could not refrain from sampling the forbidden tree. Since that earliest moment, the sin which tumbled into the world can be traced to this inability to control our desires and suppress our appetites.

Where do we find it difficult to constrain ourselves? Ruthlessly pursuing personal goals, drawing attention to our accomplishments, acquiring greater stocks of goods, pursuing sexual satisfaction, indulging in eating? Fruits which God has given us to enjoy may not be intrinsically harmful, but when we pursue them without limit or concern for God's will or regard for others, our voracity can become harmful. In sharing praise for success with a co-worker, rejoicing in the achievement of a friend, savoring the simplicity of fewer acquisitions, discovering the delights of marital fidelity, feeling better for eating well, temperance can offer unexpected blessings. Selfish indulgences seldom provide the profound pleasures which spill so generously from restraint.

Marvelous Mysteries

*M*ale butterflies of some species court their mates by secreting perfume on their wings. To mate, they hover over the female, protruding, then withdrawing a scent brush, dusting the female with perfumed powder.

The scent of the female silkworm can attract males from more than six miles away.

The honeybee queen emits an odor to attract drones on her mating flight. If you are stung by a honeybee, the residual banana scented alarm may signal other bees from the hive to attack you as well.

Salmon which have traveled thousands of miles to sea trace an odor which may have been imprinted years earlier to return to the very waters upstream where they were spawned.

Newly born mammals find their mothers' life-giving milk by smell, even before their eyes can clearly see.

Cats mark their territory and owners with their eyebrow and rump glands.

In these remarkable functions of odor, the miraculous intricacies of God's creation astound us. We cannot fail to recognize in such complex, invisible wonders the hand of God who created the vast universe, who directs all the inter-related marvels which sustain life.

Daily headlines reveal new scientific discoveries, tiny keys to unlocking secrets of the natural world. Human efforts continue to improve the quality of our lives. Yet human limitations will never uncover the unfathomable depths of God's profound wisdom. From the infinite heavens to the tiniest organism, God's magnificent orchestration inspires awe. We join David in praising God for His omniscience: "Great is the Lord and most worthy of praise; his greatness no one can fathom" (Psalm 145:3).

Sweeter Than Honey

*O*n a favorite spring stroll about the grounds of Germany's Heidelberg castle, we heard the tree ahead, alive, bee-full, roaring on the promenade. The buzz and blooming ambrosia surged and swelled in harmonic counterpoint, a poem of sound and scent.

Such buzzing industry of bees reminds us of their vital role in providing many of the fruits, vegetables, legumes, and other foods we enjoy. Insect-pollinated plants comprise approximately one third of our human diet, and eighty percent of this fertilizing is done by bees. Bee pollination yields more, larger, faster-ripening, better-tasting, and lower-priced crops. By assisting the growth of natural weeds and plants, bee pollination also prevents erosion and aids the food chain. Threatened by mites, human disturbance of habitat (not all bees nest in hives), and large agricultural tracts which lure them from native plants, bee populations are declining. We want to avoid killing them and, instead, encourage their populations with plants of season-long blooms.

Then, of course, bees also create a delicious dietary bonus—honey. To produce one pound of honey, bees may visit over two million flowers in trips over 55,000 miles. Unlike bumblebees, butterflies, and hummingbirds, which dart between various blooms, mixing pollens, honeybees extract nectar from only the one flower which is producing most nectar. Bees extract nectar with their tongues and store approximately ten times their weight in a pollen pouch to carry back to their hives. There they pass the nectar to young bees who distribute droplets throughout the honeycombs. From extraction, to storage, to transfer, enzymes break down the nectar's complex sugars into simple ones. At this stage, bees speed the evaporation of moisture from the nectar by fanning with their wings, then seal the cells with secreted wax.

This intricate manufacturing process produces honey distinctively flavored by the blossoms bees have visited. Alfalfa, buckwheat, clover, orange blossom, and tupelo are just a handful of over three hundred varieties available in the United States. Generally, lighter color equates with milder taste. Darker honeys tend to be stronger in flavor. From the floral nectars used in its creation, honey derives nutritional value in trace amounts of vitamins, minerals, and amino acids, and offers antioxidant properties as well, benefits absent from refined sugar.

Ancient Egyptians treated cuts, burns, and cataracts with honey. Greek physician Hyppocrates used it in the treatment of ulcers and skin disorders. More recently, German doctors, during World War I, dressed soldiers' wounds with a honey and cod liver oil mixture. Applying honey to minor skin abrasions, burns, and injuries appears to have been sound medicine. Honey inhibits the growth of bacteria, promotes healing, prevents scaring, and keeps bandages from sticking to wounds.

Honey has conveyed purity and sweetness in marriage traditions throughout world history. Roman brides were carried over drops of honey placed on the couple's threshold. Honey has long been an ingredient in wedding cakes and wine, marriage rites, and even appears in many languages to denote a phase of newlywed delight, the honeymoon.

In the business of bees and their bright product of golden summer is ample evidence of God's sweet provision. The Bible, too, alludes to His providence. When God called Moses to lead His chosen people, he promised to bring them to "a land flowing with milk and honey" (Exodus 3:8). God kept His promise by delivering an often disobedient nation, and demonstrated His generosity in the thriving plant and animal life of their new home. Descendent of this rescued people, the psalmist praises God for keeping His promises in Psalm 119:103: "How sweet are your words to my taste, sweeter than honey to my mouth!"

In spite of our own errant ways, God continues to fulfill His promises to us today. Going to great lengths for us, even sacrificing His only Son, God creates from the nectar of His grace the honeyed promise of salvation, which nourishes and heals us. What could be sweeter?

Autumn Aura

*L*ate marigolds finally begin to nod, leaves incline to tumble, listless grass declines, and cold rain brews all into lavish potpourri. Cast in steeping redolence, the fading season returns to us in vivid retrospective and revenance of spring.

In the height of life's summer, we often cannot appreciate the moment's radiance. Only when the colder seasons of life arrive and we reflect upon the remnant of those days do we then recall their glory. In bleaker days, distilled remembrances resonate of life's return. When we recognize that change, separation, and loss are the nature of life on this earth, we can live fully, without fearing them, and find in them the means of renewal. "Therefore we do not lose heart. Though outwardly we are wasting away, yet inwardly we are being renewed day by day" (II Corinthians 4:16).

"Praise to the Lord, O my soul, and forget not all his benefits—who forgives all your sins and heals all your diseases, who redeems your life from the pit and crowns you with love and compassion, who satisfies your desires with good things so that your youth is renewed like the eagle's" (Psalm 103:2-5).

Waking Promise

*I*n the b-r-r-r-r of January when nature seems asleep, and we would like nothing better than a nap in a warm bed ourselves, we dream of the promise of spring and the return of life. Then, while eyes are closed and mind adrift, a hint of budding pink on late winter branches steals forth. We look more closely to assure our sight. The vision is real. Dozing groves begin to bud, waiting to erupt in glorious sunshine. This slightest suggestion of life reassures us that blossoms will once more swell with color and fling their fragrant bouquets.

When we ache with unbearable loss, the scene is comforting, for Christ offers just such awakening to those who believe His promise. Like a trace on trees of sweet blossoms ahead, His words assure us: "I am the resurrection and the life. He who believes in me will live, even though he dies; and whoever lives and believes in me will never die" (John 11:25). Jesus spoke these consoling words to his friends Martha and Mary when they grieved the death of their brother. The women were distraught. Even Jesus himself could not contain his tears over the loss of his dear friend Lazarus. He asked to be taken to the tomb, commanded the stone be removed despite protestations against the stench of decay, and called forth his beloved friend. In one of the most dramatic of Jesus miracles, Lazarus walked from the tomb, still bound in grave linens. Bystanders must have had to look again to be certain their eyes were not deceiving them. Yes, they could see, Jesus had restored life to a man dead for days. The glory of God could not be denied.

None of us will escape the tears Jesus himself shed at the death of a loved one. We will feel that our heartache cannot be relieved, that our void cannot be filled, that our sadness will never end. But those buds forming imperceptibly on winter branches bear the promise of glory we have by faith in the cold face of death. Those who believe will awaken to blossom with new life in the warm and radiant presence of our Lord.

Heaven Scent

The word "perfume" originates in the Latin "per," meaning "through" and "fumum," meaning "smoke." This etymology alludes to the release of fragrance by burning scented materials, a common practice in early worship.

God gave to Moses a specific formula for incense to perfume His tabernacle (Exodus 30:34-38). Stacte, dried drops of gum which oozed from the storax tree, was processed to produce an aromatic fragrance. The musky scent of onycha, probably the horny shield of a mollusc foot, was not appealing itself, but enhanced the strength of other ingredients. Galbanum (Helbenah), the hardened sap of a common milky weed, preserved the scent of other ingredients. And frankincense, the gum of a tree, burned easily and fragrantly.

Many of the ingredients of this sacred recipe were commonplace and readily available. Often we feel the small services we perform close to home are too mundane to be as worthy as the offerings of those who serve in grander ways or in distant places. As a result, we may not be inclined to offer to perform or to give our best effort to insignificant or menial endeavors. Some of the tasks we are asked to do may even be distasteful. We might prefer to ignore or delegate them. But by evading them, or performing them half-heartedly, we miss the fragrant value they can bring to our own lives, dispense to others, and offer to God in praise.

The sight of incense's skyward smoke and the smell of its savory ascension can create a beautiful sensory impression of our petitions rising heavenward to God's throne of grace. King David asks that his prayers be acceptable in Psalm 141:2: "May my prayer be set before you like incense; may the lifting up of my hands be like the evening sacrifice."

Under Constantine the Great, the first Christian Emperor of Rome, Christianity began to flourish peaceably after centuries of persecution. At his order, Christian churches continually burned scented candles, tapers, and fragrant oil lamps, establishing the traditional use of aromatics in Church ritual. During the Reformation, by its association with ostentatious trappings of worship, burning incense fell out of some favor. But, perhaps we might re-examine the spiritual elevation of aromatic alms.

The sacred use of incense and perfumed candles is not a form of bribery that God will listen closer, or act more promptly, or respond as we desire. Rather, in raising a pleasing aroma to God with our prayers, we emphasize the sincerity of our petitions and convey our gratitude.

My husband and I often take bundles of herbs or gifts from the garden—chutney, pickles, salsa, jardinière—to restaurateur friends, not to entice better food or more attentive service, but as a token of thanks for the favor of pleasurable dining we have enjoyed with them in the past. Similarly, a perfumed invocation can demonstrate our ardent devotion, our earnest supplication, and our profound appreciation for God's bountiful goodness.

* Biblical fragrance ingredients in these essays are from the King James Version. Some ingredients are referred to by different names in later translations.

Handling Holy Oil

God gave explicit directions to the children of Israel for formulating the holy anointing oil used in the tabernacle (Exodus 30: 22-25). Although priests required a discerning sense of smell, many commoners with equally valuable, albeit less recognized, talents acquired the materials, blended the ingredients, and created the sacred oil.

The myrrh used in anointing oil required combing sticky particles from the beards of goats which grazed where the rock rose grew or tediously dragging leather thongs over the gum of broken plants. This gum was mixed with the resin scraped from an Arabian tree. The choice cinnamon and cassia from tree bark of distant commerce were carefully selected and beaten into fine powder. Sweet calamus came from dried and beaten ginger grass. (Roots of this plant were woven into window and verandah screens which scented breezes.) These ingredients were blended with olive oil, which was valued for its power to light, nourish, and heal. The mixture was ripened, strained to purity, then aged until the spices suffused the oil.

Those who gathered, traded, processed, and prepared the valued oils were common people, contributing anonymously to God's purpose in unrecognizable ways. When we offer our service to God and to others, our efforts often go unnoticed. Although our overtures, prayers, hours, or resources may seem meager or inconsequential, we know God sanctifies our efforts. In Matthew 25:40, Jesus previews the words of judgment: "Whatever you did for one of the least of these brothers of mine, you did for me." By handling His fragrant ingredients of love and charity, our acts are consecrated, and we absorb the blessing of God's fragrant emanance.

Healing Balm

*I*n Psalm 23:5 is the tender image of the shepherd anointing his sheep with oil: "You anoint my head with oil; my cup overflows." This was not likely an expensive fragrant oil, but rather a simple healing balm, like olive oil. We imagine the Biblical shepherd tenderly pouring drops from his little flask to soothe the face and body of the poor creature which had been scratched by brambles, afflicted by parasites, pursued by flies, bitten by insects, irritated by plants poisons, or wounded by attacking predators. The attentive shepherd may have mixed the oil with sulfur, spices, or herbal compounds, depending on the needs of his sheep. He may have refreshed an overheated animal with a cool drink, or shared his wine to warm a frozen one. This beloved psalm consoles us when the thorns of life tear at us, persistent hardships torment us, bad decisions plague us, and troubled relationships injure us.

Committed to memory, the psalm's soothing sentiments can be recalled at the most stressful of moments—at a deathbed, in a hospital waiting room, in a moment of meltdown. When we are physically sick or emotionally suffering, when we fear our pain will be untreatable, when we find our miseries unbearable, we often keep these concerns to ourselves to avoid burdening others, and are left feeling exhausted, alone, depressed. Well-meaning assurances and sympathetic murmurs do little to relieve our distress. At such moments, the psalmist's comforting words assure us that The Good Shepherd will enfold us tenderly in His arms, close to the warm and steady beating of His heart, anointing and healing us with His love.

Oil of Joy

"You love righteousness and hate wickedness; therefore God, your God, has set you above your companions by anointing you with the oil of joy" (Psalms 45:7).

*I*n Biblical times, anointing the head with oil was a gesture of esteem. Costly oils made from exotic fragrances of myrrh, aloes, and cassia were sealed in alabaster vases, which were then broken at the neck to apply. The valuable oils were poured lavishly over the heads of guests and spilled over robes with extravagant fragrance.

During one of Jesus' visits to the home of his friends in Bethany, Mary anointed Jesus' head and feet with the precious oil of spikenard as a precursor to his burial, then tenderly dried His feet with her hair. Some of his company complained about the wastefulness of her gesture, the cost of which, almost a year's wages for a working man, might have been given to the poor. Jesus, however, praised her generosity (John 12:1-8). Imagine how Mary's loving and adoring tribute to her Savior enveloped the room and its guests!

Mary was not intimidated by criticism or cost. She demonstrated the very essence of charity in her lavish, unrestrained gift to her Lord. True generosity permeates the heart, suffuses our being, and overflows to drench others in loving actions. If we are truly magnanimous, we will not stop to wonder how little we can get by with, what the expense will be to ourselves, how much time it will require, how the action will be perceived, how we will benefit, or whether someone else might be called upon. Rather, we will open our arms and hearts and suffuse the recipient with our selfless, sumptuous gift. With whom might we share the oil of joy?

Epiphany Essences

My husband's anniversary gift to me has become something of a tradition. He knows that a gift of my favorite perfume will always delight me, and the pleasure of its aroma returns to him. Fragrance seems an especially appropriate thoughtfulness since we were married on Epiphany. When the Magi came to worship Jesus, two of their three gifts were scent (Matthew 2:11). The gold, frankincense, and myrrh symbolize the royalty, priesthood, and humanity of the Christ child. Gold's suggestion of wealth implies His kingship; its imperishable gleam, His divinity. Frankincense, burned in religious offering, denotes His priesthood. And myrrh, offered as a painkiller at the cross and used for embalming at His burial, indicates Jesus' suffering and death.

At the height of summer's heat, frankincense and myrrh are collected from the bark of different Arabian trees by making an incision deep enough to penetrate to the trees' secretory canals. The oozing resin coagulates into blisters of yellowish myrrh and reddish-brown frankincense, which are then scraped from the trunks before seasonal rains arrive. In this hardened form, the substances were easily transported even in days when distant travel was long and arduous.

Because it flames easily and releases a balsamic odor when warmed or burned, frankincense was an ingredient of incense used by priests to convey the prayers of God's people heavenward. As one of the Magi's gifts to Jesus, it indicated that He would serve as intercessor between sinful man and God.

The Magi's gift of myrrh was used both to relieve pain and to embalm a body for burial, denoting Jesus' anguish and death. Myrrh mixed with wine was offered to Christ, but rejected, as he suffered on the cross to bear and atone for our sins (Mark 15:23). Nicodemus brought a mixture of myrrh and aloes to the tomb to help Joseph of Arimathea prepare Jesus body for burial, winding spices in the linen (John 19:39).

(As members of the Sanhedrin before which Jesus was taken during His trial, these two men did not speak in His behalf, although they secretly followed Him. Whether they failed to defend Him out of fear for themselves or doubt about His resurrection, their gesture at His grave demonstrated devotion. Was it too late? We might draw a parallel between their silence and our own reluctance in professing our faith.)

Their burial mixture of myrrh and aloes suggests the divine and human duality of Christ. While myrrh is the aromatic resin of a living tree, aloes is fragrant wood from the resinous heart of a tree cut down.* To fulfill the purpose for which God the Father had sent Him to earth, Christ had to live among mortals and even die, but Christ also manifest God's promise to return His Son to life. Both Christ's sacrifice for us in death and His living promise were interred in the garden grave. The myrrh and aloes prepared his terrestrial body for burial and his celestial body for resurrection, previewing how our own redeemed bodies will die and rise again. This act of scenting Jesus' burial shroud recognized both His manhood and His Godhood.

After the Sabbath, early Sunday morning, women close to Jesus arrived at the garden tomb with spices and perfumes to anoint His body (Luke 24:1). Do you suppose that among their aromatics may have been the original myrrh which the Magi had given to Jesus as a child? I like to think that Mary may have kept this precious gift, pondering God's plan, recognizing that her Son may give His life as Savior and Messiah of His people.

The wonder and significance of this morning, of course, is that the women found their spices unnecessary. In an empty tomb and the message "He is risen" (Luke 24:2-8), the salvation promise of the Christ child was fulfilled.

* A popular belief holds that this Aquilaria agallocha is the sole tree descended from the Garden of Eden, referred to as "Paradise wood."

Extracting a Fragrant Spirit

*A*lthough the rosemary in our herb patch releases its fragrance without coaxing, thyme must be bruised, bay leaves broken, and oregano brushed against to emit their scents. Working among our herbs, kneeling on some plants, rubbing against others, snapping a few stems unintentionally, provokes a sublime effusion of scents. Many aromatic substances— flowers, brackets, pods, leaves, stems, kernels, seeds, bark, wood, roots, rhizomes, mosses, gums, and sap—may be crushed, heated, pressed, or variously handled to render their fragrances.

To extract nectars for perfume, considerable processing is required. Enfleurage is an older technique, seldom used today, whereby petals were painstakingly layered on fat-coated glass plates. When the fat absorbed the scent, it was processed to render oil. Expression simply uses pressure to extract such oils as citrus. Distillation requires boiling petals in water and condensing the steam to produce an oil. In extraction, used for more delicate flowers which cannot be subject to high heat, the oils, waxes, and pigments of petals are dissolved on metal plates submerged in solvent. The mixture is evaporated, then dissolved in alcohol and filtered to produce a concentrated essence.

Similarly, God may reveal His lessons and blessings to us through trial and sorrow. Suffering is integral to living, unavoidable. When we are crushed in the daily grind, broken by overwhelming hardship, pressured by demands, bruised by struggle, God extracts from these challenges a fragrant spirit. We come to recognize our own insufficiency and to acknowledge our dependence on God. The essence which emerges from burden and distress is often a more intimate relationship with Him, which results in healing, comfort, and hope. Our situation may not change, our troubles may not disappear, but God does promise help to confront our difficulties and strength to withstand. In enduring assault and affliction, the apostle Paul found, "Suffering produces perseverance; perseverance, character; and character, hope" (Romans 5:3-4). Hope is not merely wishing; it is rather assurance based on evidence of God's past provision. His hope promises not just relief, but a confident peace. Paul testifies to God's faithfulness in the most trying circumstances: "I can do everything through him who gives me strength" (Philippians 4:13).

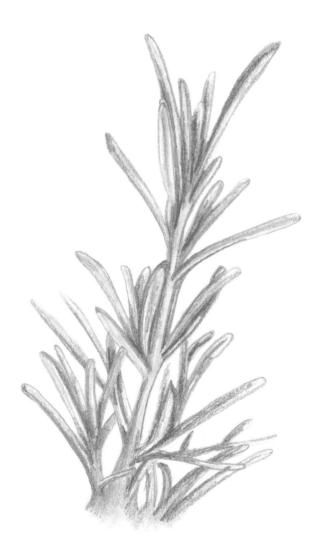

Notable Ingredients

*C*reating a perfume may require four or five hundred ingredients or "notes" of over two thousand currently available. Some characteristic odors include floral (jasmine, rose, lily of the valley, gardenia), spicy (carnation, cinnamon, nutmeg, cloves), woody (sandalwood, cedar), mossy (oak moss), herbal (clover, sweet grass, lavender, basil), fruity (citrus, pear, apple, berry), and leather (leather, tobacco, birch tar). Within these categories, variations exist. A rose note, for instance, may be Bulgarian, French, Moroccan, Turkish, synthetic, or a blend.

Some notes actually smell foul. Who would imagine secretions from species of wildcat (civet), beaver (castoreum), or deer (musk) would be sought as perfume ingredients? Yet, in small amounts, these elements can make a fragrance voluptuous and lasting. Today these notes are often synthetic to protect endangered animals and to ensure greater consistency of odor.

Perfumers create a complex composition based on the evaporation rate of selected ingredients. The top or head note is the first released by the skin. In Chanel No. 5, for example, it is a bright synthetic aldehyde, which smells like starched laundry. The middle note, or heart, establishes the character of the fragrance, and lasts for hours. Finally, the bottom note, or dry down, often animal scent, provides a depth of fragrance which can linger for days.

To create a single ingredient, an enormous volume of the original substance is required. The entire harvest of great fields of French jasmine, for instance, is reduced to only a few tons of absolute. Sixty thousand rose blossoms produce only one ounce of rose oil. When hundreds of exotic ingredients are combined, we begin to see why perfumes command the prices they do. Orris, for example, from an iris rhizome, sells for $40,000 a pound! Yet no single ingredient can be considered more valuable than another when each brings its distinctive quality to the perfumer's composition.

As individual members of the body of Christ, we also have personal qualities which no one else can duplicate. I Corinthians 12:4-6 explains: "There are different kinds of gifts, but the same Spirit. There are different kinds of service, but the same Lord. There are different kinds of working, but he same God works in all men." Few of us can claim to be capable in every capacity, including the Martha Stewarts among us who imply anyone can be competent in everything.

Even to gardening, we bring different talents. We may prefer designing landscapes, collecting perennials, nurturing roses, establishing shade gardens, or experimenting with color. At work, we may be good at organizing, attentive to details, or gifted with people. Comparing our talents with those of others not only is pointless, but can be damaging. Focusing on someone else's superior quality in one aspect can make us feel inferior or jealous. Instead, we need to consider the gifts God has given to each of us personally and search for the ways in which we may put those skills and talents to use in His service—whether it is nurturing families, organizing activities, creating music or art, conducting business, volunteering, teaching, leading, offering encouragement, demonstrating compassion, providing financial support, or being an attentive listener. Our efforts can contribute in a variety of meaningful ways, as I Peter 4:10 suggests: "Each one should use whatever gift he has received to serve others, faithfully administering God's grace in its various forms."

Who can say whether the vanilla or the carnation note in a fragrance is most essential to a perfume? Both are necessary to create its pleasing bouquet. It is important only that we cultivate our God-given talents to make the most fragrant contribution possible.

Fragrant Fixative

Sperm whales secrete a substance to protect their intestinal lining from the sharp bones of the cuttlefish they eat. The regurgitated waxy mass may float into fishing nets or land on shore. This dense brown lump is the prized ambergris, used as a fixative in perfume. Its earthy smell develops a hint of violets. Other common fixatives include gum benzoin, calamus root, frankincense, myrrh, oak moss, orris root, tonka beans, vetivert root, civet, and musk. A fixative stabilizes a fragrance to prevent its rapid evaporation and to keep it from changing. In effect, it captures the scent and secures it.

As with perfumes, our relationships require the assurance that they are fixed or lasting. When love truly binds us, even in moments of misunderstanding or unkindness, we know those trying moments will pass. We look for ways to resolve our conflicts and reassure one another of our loyalty.

I Corinthians 13:4-8 gives us the following advice: "Love is patient, love is kind. It does not envy, it does not boast, it is not proud. It is not rude, it is not self-seeking, it is not easily angered, it keeps no record of wrongs. Love does not delight in evil but rejoices with the truth. It always protects, always trusts, always hopes, always perseveres. Love never fails." Those words can be hard to practice consistently even in the best relationships. Patience and kindness require putting the needs of another before our own, often when we seem to have the least time or inclination to do so. Love can mean teeth marks on our tongues to restrain unsolicited or regretful words.

The limits imposed by relationships give us assurance. Children want guidelines, difficult though they can be to enforce, which show them that the responsibility we bear in relationships are motivated by love. While marriage bonds impose restriction, they also confirm commitment. Love refrains from control, but engenders respect in allowing latitude. Such trust, encouragement, and support will return to us in a loving relationship.

The bonds of a fragrant love are fixed—firmly held, dependable, and enduring.

A Changed Expression

*P*erfume is all about evaporation. A scent which simply seeded into the skin would be useless. In order to be enjoyed, fragrance must be converted into a vapor. Only then can it be released into the air where it can be detected. So it is with faith. Without demonstrating how our belief changes our lives, we cannot convey its importance to others. All our church going, Bible reading, and praying is of little value if we do not translate it into action. Jesus tells us in Matthew 5:16, "Let your light shine before men, that they may see your good deeds and praise your Father in heaven."

Unbelievers can be dissuaded from pursuing religion by what they perceive as hypocrisy. If the same neighbor who returns from church on Sunday morning is not distinguished as Christian by speech, action, or attitude, what is the point of faith? We need to reveal the transforming aroma of redemption in our behavior. Romans 12:2 exhorts us, "Do not conform any longer to the pattern of this world, but be transformed by the renewing of your mind. Then you will be able to test and approve what God's will is—his good, pleasing, and perfect will." Christians are invited to change as we grow spiritually. We are no longer identified by the accumulation of our past performances or failures, but daily renewed by the Holy Spirit.

No amount of perfume can cover the repellent stench of our sinful human tendencies. But, imbued by the Spirit, we can relinquish our bad habits, selfishness, grudges, bitterness, and prejudice; receive forgiveness; and express to others the marvelous essence of our salvation.

Imagine That!

erturbed that his rose perfume, La Rose Jacqueminot, was not selling, Francois Coty is said to have struck a bottle, which broke on the floor of a Parisian department store, flooding the air with its scent. In 1905, his advertising may have been unintentional, but it lured customers to ask for the perfume. Soon his stylish and innovative fragrances were commissioned by such luminaries as the czar and czarina of Russia.

Coty had a keenly discriminating olfactory sense and had steeped himself in the knowledge of perfume materials and production. He was also attentive to quality in packaging and presentation, collaborating with glassmaker Rene Lalique in creating beautiful Art Nouveau flacons, and carefully selecting paper and printing of labels and boxes. Coty enlarged his market by distributing samples and selling smaller bottles to customers who could not previously afford perfume.

The interest in fashionable fragrance declined with the War of 1914, but was revived after the war by couture designers. Gabrielle (Coco) Chanel was perhaps one of the period's most innovative couturiers. Her streamlined simplicity and influences borrowed from male fashion were reflected in her trademark perfume Numero Cinq (Chanel Number Five). Packaged in a manly rectangular bottle, labeled in spare black and white, the sharp aldehydic floral was a departure from previous softly sweet fragrances.

The secret of such innovators as Coty and Chanel was imagination. While they did not formulate their perfumes themselves, they envisioned new concepts, styles, approaches, manifestations, and presentations of their products. Perfumers themselves require creativity to compose the new fragrances they envision. Then the bottle, box, label, advertising, and distribution, must also inventively distinguish the product in the market. Imagination is critical throughout the development of a fragrance, from design to sales.

In our own personal development, it is often a lack of imagination which causes many of the difficulties we encounter. When we confront seemingly insurmountable conflicts with others or problems we are unable to resolve, we are quick to apply conventional and comfortable approaches which we have used in the past, regardless of whether they have been productive or not.

When we disagree with a spouse, we fall comfortably into past patterns of behavior, forgetting how unfruitful raised voices, obstinacy, repetition, or criticism have been in similar confrontations. When our point of view differs from that of a colleague, misunderstandings result because we find it difficult to take any perspective but our own. When a committee recommends new options, we hamper progress by balking at unfamiliar innovations which have not been tried before. When we are faced with a challenge we cannot seem to overcome, we keep trying to resolve it with modes of thinking which still don't work, complaining and worrying about the persistence of the problem.

These are all occasions when we might benefit from applying more imagination. Marital disharmony might be soothed by listening truly attentively to a spouse's concern, examining our own fault in the quarrel, distasteful though that is, and considering how we might alter our own behavior, rather than insisting that our partner change. Offering reconciliation instead of stubbornly demanding our own way will more likely result in a compatible solution and encourage a more generous spirit in our spouse as well.

Differences in approach on the job are more likely to be resolved when we make a real effort to see the reasoning behind a co-worker's idea, rather than simply rejecting it because it differs from our own. Keeping the end purpose of a project in mind may help us to focus on similarities in outcome rather than on differences in approach, to reconcile divergent perspectives. Stepping outside our own mindset and agenda can be uncomfortable and is seldom easy, but a spirit of cooperation is contagious.

Change is challenging. We tend to cling to familiar behavior, ideas, and patterns in relationships. New proposals can make our hair stand on end and cause us to criticize anything different. Imagination means open-mindedness. Creativity can inject energy and momentum when a work, church, family, or individual goal seems stuck or unattainable.

When we seem constantly to be struggling with the same issues which cause us persistent anguish and despair, imagination is sorely needed. This means recognizing that the excuses we have been making have become stumbling blocks. Forcing ourselves to act, to seek help, to commit, to sally forth requires overcoming inertia, self-pity, and confronting the challenge with fresh eyes. Our body will not become fit, our relationship will not mend, our work situation will not improve, our outlook on life will not change unless we deliberately strive to alter our present state or seek the help to do so.

Imagination is vital to wisdom. Informed by knowledge and intellect, wisdom is the application of creative solutions to the perplexing decisions. When Solomon was uncertain about how to confront his responsibilities, he asked God for help. God responded by giving Solomon wisdom and insight, which he used in deciding two women's claim to the same baby. This tactic required imagination (I Kings 3:4-28).

The more often we make an effort to consciously apply imagination and seek God's help in this difficult enterprise, the more successful we will be in making wise choices and fashioning the fragrant life we desire. Imagine the prospect!

Graceful Containers

As we stroll through enticing displays of department store perfumes, elegant shapes and glittering glass enhance shimmering liquid and invite us to caress bottles even before we sniff the aromatics inside. Perfume marketers know that much of the appeal of perfume is the container. Curvaceous contours, chiseled facets, gold closures and embellishments reveal the amber, coral, crystal, lapis, and emerald contents, like aqueous jewels.

To secure it from evaporation and contamination, costly fine perfume has always been secured in an appropriately beautiful receptacle. Ancient Egyptian bath oils, unguents, and perfumes were held in artful alabaster, glass, earthenware, and faience containers. In Asia, Egypt, Rome, Arabia, and Italy, glass became the vessel of choice. The classical world stored fragrances in artful ceramic containers. Porcelain was a popular material in China for holding scent.

In God's eyes, we are precious vessels, filled with His Spirit. II Timothy 2:21 reminds us that each person God claims as His own "shall be a vessel unto honor, sanctified, and meet for the master's use, and prepared unto every good work" (KJV).

We are the creation of the master craftsman who has designed us to decant His priceless grace in an often oblivious and hostile world. He has made us both valuable and responsible.

How do we keep the content of our souls inviolable and yet apply it in a world which seeks to contaminate and deplete our spiritual resources? Although we like to deny the influence, what we expose ourselves to does indeed affect us. The television and movies we watch, the books and periodicals we read, the web sites we visit, the company we keep, the places we go, the pastimes we pursue, the thoughts we entertain, all have subtle effects on our sanctity. If we think we can avoid the insidious repercussions of ill-chosen or immoral involvements on our spiritual well-being and personal behavior, we deceive ourselves.

We cannot apply God's priceless grace as He has directed when it has been diluted or defiled by the world. Although avoiding such appealing assaults is a persistent and difficult challenge, preserving our consecration is worth the effort. Philippians 4:8 advises, "Whatever is true, whatever is noble, whatever is right, whatever is pure, whatever is lovely, whatever is admirable—if anything is excellent or praiseworthy—think about such things."

The words of Thomas Moore convey the sacred resonance of our spiritual essence: "You may break, you may shatter the vase, if you will,/ But the scent of the roses will hang round it still." We need to remind ourselves that our bodies, minds, and spirits are the art of God. We want our containers to indicate sanctity within, to pour forth evidence of God's invaluable grace in our lives.

What's In a Name?

Boudoir, Clandestine, Divine Folie, Indiscret, Intoxication d' Amour, J'Adore, No Regrets, Oh la la, Perhaps, Private Number, Secret de Venus, Shocking, Tabu, Touch. Such perfume names are selected to seduce us into imagining passionate prospects. Others suggest exotic escapes to the jungle, beach, casbah, countryside, or metropolis— Animale, Eau Fresh, Samsara, Blue Grass, Montana, Tuscany, Paris, Fifth Avenue. Some promise the qualities for which we yearn—Joy, Pleasure, Sensation. Others allude to association with royalty or celebrity—Miss Dior, Diva, Princess Grace. Particularly popular recently are fragrances offering the cachet of designer names— Coco, Lauren, KL. Recognizing the importance of a name to a perfume's appeal, perfumers often reserve and register fragrance names years in advance, even before a product is developed, to assure exclusive use of an appellation.

The name we received at baptism is equally vital to our spiritual identity. We are called Christians for our namesake Christ—the Messiah, the Savior, the Holy One.

As Christians we become the daughters and sons of God, the sisters and brothers of Christ. Our designation as Christians commits us to upholding that name, just as our devotion to an earthly family prevents us from behaving in any manner that would besmirch or embarrass the head of our family or other family members who share that name. We are, in effect, representatives of the virtues our family unit values, and we want to exemplify the family's integrity. Our name as Christians reminds us of our responsibility to preserving the sanctity of that name and to honoring our namesake, Jesus Christ.

Our Christian name means that we are claimed as God's own children. "How great is the love the Father has lavished on us, that we should be called children of God" (I John 3:1)! The assurance of II Timothy 2:19, "The Lord knows those who are His," makes us responsive to His voice when He speaks to us personally in His Word. He calls us His loved ones; provides for our needs; offers us salvation; and, by recording our names in the Book of Life, invites us to share His company eternally. What more could a name offer?

Selecting Scent

*H*ow do you choose a new perfume? Do you buy a brand which is currently popular? Ask a friend for the name of an appealing fragrance she is wearing? Sniff scents from a department store cosmetic counter until they seem indistinguishable? Look for a pretty bottle? Fall for a tantalizing name? Succumb to advertising promises?

I used to attempt any and all of the above techniques until we spent time in France. Frenchwomen seem to waft self-assured style in their wake of fluttering scarves and scent. Even in small villages, the parfumerie is often the setting where ladies congregate to chat and socialize while occupied with the serious matter of personal fragrance selection.

Shortly after our return to America, I found the personalized approach to perfume which I had sought in one of our favorite destinations, Charleston, South Carolina. Pegge Schall and Ashley Futeral, mother and daughter proprietresses of the House of Versailles, possess encyclopedic knowledge of perfumes, their components and histories; an extensive fragrance library; and a large inventory of hard-to-find perfumes. In a personal consultation, they inquired about my preferences and tested for pH to determine fragrances most compatible with my body chemistry. I then ranked various fragrance categories sampled on my skin (intermittently sniffing coffee grounds to neutralize previous scents). After narrowing preferences, the ladies made recommendations within the selected fragrance families and assisted in selecting perfumes which best suit me, keeping notes on my choices for reference on return visits.

Exploring fragrance in these ladies' informed and charming company over the years, I have indulged my interest in learning about the nuances of scent. Even my wine tasting seems to grow more discriminating, and I am beginning to understand why our French sommelier friend found her second calling in the perfume business. Now the fragrances I wear truly reflect who I am.

The experience has made me consider how infrequently other choices we make may truly reflect who we are. What criteria do we commonly use in the choices we make? Do we buy into current codes of appropriate behavior rather than adhere to God's rules for morality? Do we behave as we do because everyone else does? Have we blurred the lines of acceptable conduct until we don't really recognize sin? Do we act as we do to feel accepted by others? Do we think that by choosing the ways of the world we will finally find happiness? Do we even know what criteria to apply to the choices we make? Perhaps we find choices difficult because we do not truly know ourselves.

As His children, God's words of instruction for our lives help us to determine appropriate choices, lead us to preferences in keeping with His will, offer recommendations for fitting selections, and promise continued guidance whenever we return to Him for help. Ephesians 1:4 reminds us that "He chose us in him before the creation of the world to be holy and blameless in his sight." By exploring our choices with God, the perfume of our lives will truly reflect who we are, His chosen.

Splashing Scent

*I*f a fragrance is particularly treasured, we may be inclined to save it for special occasions, doling it out in meager drops. But a perfume used so sparingly is likely to provide little enjoyment. And if left in the bottle on a dresser too long, the scent may eventually evaporate or turn unpleasant. The pleasure of perfume is in its wearing. In the words of Estee Lauder, "Perfume is like love. You can never get enough of it."

So it is with our faith. We cannot know its meaning for our lives until we apply it to the circumstances of living, using it to guide, console, and uplift us. Only by using and sharing our faith can we savor the essence of God's blessings. His promises are not just for Sundays, or the hereafter; they are for lavish splashing anytime. "How great is the love the Father has lavished on us, that we should be called children of God! And that is what we are!" (I John 3:1).

Door to Door

*I*n more innocent times, when doors opened easily, invitingly, door-to-door solicitation was a popular means of selling vacuum cleaners, encyclopedias, brushes, and perhaps most memorably, Avon. A New York bookseller founded the perfume company when he discovered customers were buying his books for the rose oil perfumes he was giving away. He later named his company for Stratford-on-Avon, birthplace of his favorite playwright, William Shakespeare. Shortly thereafter, the company's direct sales were pioneered.

When the door bell rang, three girls in our household joined Mother to answer the Avon lady's familiar chirrup, hoping for tiny lip color samples and miniature perfume vials with transporting names: Here's My Heart, Cotillion, Persian Wood, Somewhere, To a Wild Rose, Unforgettable, Topaze. Lip colors which did not suit Mother found their way into our bathroom-counter beauty parlor for dolls, who were subject to so much shampooing, hair styling, and make-up experiment that their original hair and coloring were ruined beyond recognition.

The Avon ladies we knew were more than saleswomen; they often knit disparate elements of a community by bearing neighborhood news and inquiring about our own family. One charitable Avon representative on our block and her husband ministered later in life as hospice caregivers to my dear aunt suffering from Alzheimer's, dabbing her with scent, massaging her hands with fragrant lotions, applying colorful nail polish. This thoughtfulness seemed particularly appropriate to my aunt, who often allowed us as children to play freely with the perfumes and powders on her mirrored dressing table. Although Alzheimer's patients often lose their sense of smell as the disease progresses and doors of perception close in the mind, my aunt surely knew comfort and solace in those warm touches, gentle kindnesses, and tender gestures.

Care of the sick or dying, while often thrust upon us, is a task few of us wish to assume. It requires great measures of patience, compassion, and selflessness, qualities which are seldom humanly sufficient without coming to the door of God for divine help.

He reminds us in our reluctance, that by helping those in need, we offer this evidence of love and service to God Himself (Matthew 25:31-46).

Fragrant Inheritance

*I*n New Orleans' French Quarter at 824 Royal Street, the historic Dejan House is home to Hové Parfumeur. In the cool, aromatic interior, rich wood, elegant mirrors, and antique furnishings of the 1813 residence evoke images of ladies in floor-length silk and fine feathered millinery. Enduring essences with enchanting names—Imperatrice, Vous Souvenez-Vous, Belle Chasse—and soaps of southern scent—Tea Olive, Vetivert, and Magnolia—are created on the premises. While sniffing testers, one may catch a glimpse of the back lab where inherited formulas are still used in products today.

The business was begun in 1931 by Mrs. Alvin Hovey-King, the daughter of a Cavalry officer, who learned the art of perfume making from her Creole French mother. When the investment business of her retired Navy Commander husband was ruined in the market crash of 1929, Mrs. Hovey-King developed her pastime into a business with the help of her daughter. Eventually Mrs. Hovey-King's granddaughter and her husband assumed the tradition. The family's occupation with fragrance is maintained today through several generations.

What will we pass on through generations of our families? Could any inheritance be more enduring or sustaining than the love of God? Since children are likely to value what their parents have demonstrated to be important, early years in church and Sunday school are especially vital to spiritual nurturing. Jesus emphasizes the importance of this responsibility: "Let the little children come to me, and do not hinder them, for the kingdom of God belongs to such as these" (Mark 10:14).

If parents cannot agree on which faith to emphasize, or do not find religion important themselves, they may be inclined to do nothing and allow children to develop their own interest in religion when they are older. But if children have not been introduced to God, how will they recognize a spiritual void? Some may come to faith as adults, but they will have missed the years of grounding which could have enriched their spiritual growth. Learning French, or the perfume business, or God's love can certainly be more effective when begun early.

What spiritual legacy are we leaving our children?

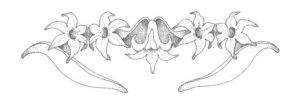

Aromatic Adornment

*I*n ancient Egypt, wax cones of unguent worn on the head slowly melted to imbue the hair and head with scent. Greek and Roman women filled urn-shaped earrings with perfume, which spilled over their shoulders as they moved. In Eastern countries, resins and botanicals were worn in brooches, gems, and rings. Various cultures throughout history have worn beads of perfumed paste, which yielded their aroma when warmed by the body. Today I wear a bracelet of antique buttons from my husband, to which I have added one padded button for perfuming. Throughout history, the appeal of fragrant embellishments has endured.

The importance of scented accents and apparel are understandable when we consider that until recent history, plumbing was absent, bathing inaccessible, clothing difficult if not impossible to wash, and animals close companions. Nosegays have been adapted to fashions through the years on dresses, jackets, hats, fans, and muffs to ward off stenches.

Fragrant pomanders, which assuaged the odors and pestilence of medieval streets, evolved during the fifteenth century into gold and silver receptacles worn around the neck or at the waist as fashion accessories. In later eras of constricting corsets, decorative vessels containing vinegar, herbs, and spices served as fainting aids as well.

Jewelry has not been the only popular aromatic adornment. Alexander the Great soaked his tunics in saffron. Spanish leathers saturated with a citrus, rose, and musk perfume, adapted from the Moorish tradition encountered during the Crusades, were made into shoes, jerkins, cloaks, and other aristocratic clothing during Elizabethan times. Eighteenth century European ladies favored folding fans of sandalwood, the better to waft their allure. In the new world, Creole women of Louisiana preferred the vetiver fan of ancient India. Intricately designed Indian shawls of fine cashmere became popular in England and Europe during the early nineteenth century for their scent of patchouli leaves, which protected the handiwork from insects in shipment.

Isaiah 61:10 describes the adornments we wear as Christians: "I will greatly rejoice in the Lord, my soul shall be joyful in my God; for he hath clothed me with the garments of salvation, he hath covered me with the robe of righteousness, as a bridegroom decketh himself with ornaments, and as a bride adorneth herself with her jewels" (KJV). What could better impart to our own lives and convey to others the aroma of joy than these treasured and beautiful gifts of God?

I Peter 3:4 reminds us that outward embellishment is of little value, "But let it be the hidden man of the heart, in that which is not corruptible, even the ornament of a meek and quiet spirit, which is in the sight of God of great price" (KJV).

Acceptable Appearance

*I*n eighteenth century France, fashionable ladies applied a foundation plaster of white clay, ground pearls, honey, gum, and often, despite the warning of medical professionals, white lead. Combined with white lard and essential oils of violets, jasmine, or lilies of the valley, the mixture was used to conceal wrinkles. Rouge was created from talc, cochineal, olive oil, gum, and rosewater, then applied with a brush.

Beauty spots cut from black or purple fabric, were dipped in scent, then stuck on the cheeks, breasts, or other provocative places with gum. While initially applied to cover blemishes, the tiny patches soon became fashion statements, their placement conveying the wearer's moods and intentions as discreet, passionate, or coquettish.

In enclosed powder rooms, gentlemen and ladies wore dust cloths to protect clothing and held cone-shape masks over their faces while a mixture of talc and essential oils, especially violet-scented orris root, were sifted through silk screens or applied with bellows onto their lightly pomaded wigs.

What a lot of bother for appearance! We may not make such lavish and time-consuming use of cosmetics and hair dressing, but we often go to considerable lengths to make ourselves appealing to God. We may demonstrate our piety, make a show of good works, rationalize our omissions, excuse our misdeeds, or conceal our offenses, all in attempts to convince God that we are worthy of His love.

Our efforts, however, neither impress nor repel God. He sees through our masks, our pretenses, our camouflage, to our sinful souls and offers us unencumbered forgiveness regardless. How comforting it is to be recognized and accepted as His redeemed. "The Lord knows those who are His" (II Timothy 2:19).

If we do not acknowledge God's offer of redemption, we are destined to feel lacking, for nothing we can do will be sufficient to earn self respect or the approval of others. As a result, self-esteem appears to be in dwindling supply. In an effort to recapture it, many seek self-worth in plastic surgery, social climbing, recreational drugs, dependent relationships, personal aggrandizement, and such artificial boosters, which can compound dissatisfaction. Excessive or misguided emphasis on self-esteem often comes at the expense of personal responsibility. We become quick with excuse, blame, and deceit.

Our own efforts to feel worthy are bound to be deficient. Our value as individuals cannot derive from ourselves, but must rather come from God, who calls us to be His own. We hear His comforting words in I Peter 2:9: "But you are a chosen people, a royal priesthood, a holy nation, a people belonging to God, that you may declare the praises of him who called you out of darkness into his wonderful light." God reassures us that in His eyes we appear beautiful indeed.

Rosemary Remembrance

he principal ingredient of the first alcoholic perfume, Hungary Water, was a distillation of rosemary. The garden provided additional ingredients: grape spirit, balm, lemon peel, mint, rose, and orange flower. Until this time, perfumes were primarily in powder form. It is said that a hermit gave the recipe to Queen Elizabeth of Hungary in 1370, promising it would preserve her beauty into old age. It must have worked, as the King of Poland proposed to the queen when she was seventy-two years old. The fragrance is still produced today, used primarily as a face wash and, with rosemary's muscle soothing property, as a bath tonic.

Queen Anne of England particularly enjoyed rosemary, heating a rosemary and sugar powder to scent her rooms. In Elizabethan times, bodies of the dead were decorated with rosemary because of its lasting freshness and antiseptic properties. A distillation of rosemary seeds and flowers was drunk on rising and retiring to sweeten the breath. Rosemary was rubbed into hair to encourage its growth and luster and used in wash water to freshen clothes and linens.

For its power to stimulate mind and body, rosemary water was once purported to be the "elixir of life." Rosemary water was a principal ingredient of Eau de Cologne (along with neroli, bergamot, and lavender), which Napoleon lavished over his head and shoulders while at court and carried in his boot to assuage the stench of battle. (Its alcohol from a highly rectified grape spirit was not denatured and could be ingested as liquor a well.)

In ancient Greece, students sharpened their minds by tucking sprigs of fresh rosemary behind their ears. Rosemary's aromatic oils can increase blood flow to the brain, improving memory and mental clarity. The steam of dried rosemary tea can have a similar effect.

Perhaps students today would do well to sip a cup before exams or to dab some rosemary essential oil on a sleeve to sniff discreetly.

For its connotations of loyalty and fidelity, rosemary has long held a meaningful place in weddings: in the bride's bouquet or in her hair garland, strewn in procession, worn by the groom's attendants, and steeped in the shared cup of wine.

In an old Anglican custom dating back to the seventeenth century, mourners at funerals received sprigs of rosemary, denoting remembrance. The herb's significance no doubt alludes to the plant's persistence and longevity. An old rosemary bush may become quite woody, but can last for decades. We see evidence of its endurance in our own herb garden, where rosemary remains green all winter midst the skeletons of its sleeping neighbors, providing a continual supply of its aromatic leaves throughout the year. My husband extends the use of even dried rosemary prunings, soaking, then burning them to smoke savory grilled fish.

Rosemary reminds me of the words of Psalm 102:11-12: "My days are like a shadow that declineth; and I am withered like grass. But thou, O Lord, shalt endure forever; and thy remembrance unto all generations" (KJV). While our bodies may deteriorate and die, like the remnants of last year's plants in the garden, God will remain for all the seasons of man's habitation on this earth and beyond. In His persistent presence, God's infinite love endures.

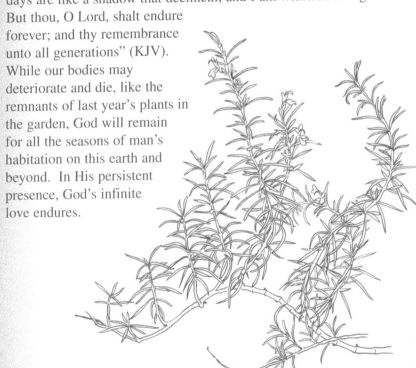

Imparting Immunity

L aboratory workers of Grasse, France, where perfume oils are extracted from flowers, are said to be notably immune to respiratory diseases. An investigation into the phenomenon discovered that the essential oils of some flowers and plants do, in fact, have curative and prophylactic properties. Experiments found yellow-fever organisms, typhoid and tuberculosis bacillus destroyed by such oils as cinnamon, clove, lavender, verbena, patchouli, angelica, valerian, juniper, sandal, and cedar.

When the tomb of Egyptian King Tutankhamen, dating from 1350 B. C., was opened in 1922, one of the perfumes found still faintly fragrant in burial vases after three thousand years was valerian. Perhaps in a time of typhoid's devastation, ancient Egyptians were aware of valerian's medicinal qualities. It may be that the use of fumigants, pomanders, unguents, mendicants, and even dietary ingredients throughout history has been informed by more than tradition or superstition.

As a palliative against the Plague of the Black Death in fourteenth and fifteenth century Europe, fires of pine, fir, and other scented woods were lit in the streets. Sulfur flowers thrown onto the flames burned the eyes, nose, and throat with acrid smoke. Tobacco imported from the New World was also introduced to prevent infection. Physicians wore long leather coats rubbed with honey-scented bees wax and high, thick gloves to avoid contamination. Masks with glass windows and beaks filled with fresh herbs, dried flower petals, or aromatic vinegars covered their heads. Canes used to transmit a pulse from an axilla or groin to the physician's ear often contained an end chamber filled with scented unguents. If a physician must touch the patient, his other hand would hold to his nose sandalwood boxes or cloth sachets filled with amber, incense, and sulfur. Preceding the physician through the streets, an assistant carried a torch which burned charcoal, resinous gums, and fragrant herbs. Houses of the dead were sprinkled about with aromatic waters, one of which survives today as Eau de Cologne. Apothecaries sold pastilles, perfumes, balsamics, drugs, herbs, salts, spirits, and other aromatics to protect against the pestilence. Lavender bunches were tied to the wrist; wormwood hung from rafters. All these preparations and practices were based in the belief, valid or not, that aromatics destroyed disease in the air. Pennyroyal and other pungent herbs were strewn in beds and on floors among rushes to prevent the spread of plague by fleabite.

Fortunately God has conquered the virulence of sin. Because we are human, sin still contaminates our attempts to obey His will, but it can no longer destroy our souls. In His death and resurrection, Christ quelled the deadly power of evil. He purified our diseased souls and removed the guilt which would have damned us. We need not purchase elaborate drug-store preparations. Immunity is easily acquired: "If we confess our sins, he is faithful and just and will forgive us our sins and purify us from all unrighteousness" (I John 1:9).

Inviting Rooms

oth Napoleon and his Empress Josephine lavishly perfumed themselves and their quarters. Josephine was particularly fond of the fragrance of violets, wearing the perfume, and growing violet scented mignonette in pots to scent her rooms. Recognizing her pleasure in violets, Napoleon had sent her the seed from his campaign in Egypt, carpeted her grave with violets when she died, and wore in exile a locket containing violets from her grave. They used other fragrances extravagantly as well. In revenge for Napoleon's annulment of their marriage in favor of a new consort, Josephine saturated her rooms at Malmaison in the heavy musk Napoleon detested. Workmen refurbishing Josephine's imperial apartments after her death found the walls so permeated with musk that they were overcome by nausea and fainting. When Napoleon died on St. Helena, vapors of incense infused his room.

While today we may scent our rooms with sprays and warmed essential oils, the ancient practice of incense burning was popular in eighteenth century England and Europe. Elaborate pastille burners perfumed rooms with fragrant smoke and banished the odors of previous courses while diners enjoyed desert. And, of course, scented candles have long been popular. Early North American settlers made them by scalding berries of the wax-myrtle and collecting wax as it surfaced. Formed into cakes, the tallow burned with little smoke and an aromatic odor.

During the Middle Ages, in wealthy churches and the halls of kings and knights, floors were strewn with rushes and herbs to sweeten the air as they were crushed underfoot. Herbs were rubbed on furniture, oak floors, and paneling, to polish and scent them.

Ancient Romans luxuriated in roses. Rose water bubbled from fountains and baths. Rose petals released from canopies showered banquet guests and covered floors feet deep. Doves with perfumed wings scented the air. Cushions and pillows were filled with dried petals.

In some eastern countries, the rhizomatous roots used in vetivert perfume were woven into sun-blinds. Watered in the heat of the day, they released a violet fragrance to scent and cool indoor rooms.

Even ancient architecture incorporated scent. Walls, beams, paneling, and entire palaces were often constructed of cedarwood, whose resinous scent repelled insects and brightened the air. Builders of ancient mosques mixed saffron, musk, and rosewater into mortar, which perfumed the air as walls were warmed by the sun.

What essences infuse the chambers of our hearts? 1 John 4:13 says, "We know that we live in him and he in us, because he has given us of his Spirit." Does the stench of our selfishness and greed repel the Spirit, or does an aura of kindness and charity invite His presence? Could God find a fragrant dwelling place in us?

Sweet Sleep

*A*round the world for centuries people have enjoyed a fragrant environment for sleep. "I have perfumed my bed with myrrh, aloes, and cinnamon," invites the lover in Proverbs 7:15-18. Mayans placed fragrant barks and herbs among their linen. In the Orient, jasmine flowers were draped over the bed at night to refresh a stale atmosphere.

Bundles of lavender and mint are similarly used in European bedrooms and sickrooms to absorb heat, mask odors, and cleanse the air with vaporous ozone. Pots of lavender on window sills and lavender buds strewn among bed linens also serve to sweeten sleeping rooms while keeping moths and vermin at bay.

In Elizabethan England, muslin bags of rosemary seeds were hung in bedrooms to induce sound slumber. Small pillows can easily be filled with chamomile, hops, lemon balm, and other relaxing garden herbs to invite rest.

While living in the country with my family, I savored the slumberous pleasures of open windows. In the silent dark, lilting breezes stirred the curtains, bearing pulses of freshly plowed earth, the languid wail of distant coyotes, and soft pools of moonlight on bedcovers.

Sleep has a sublime way of giving problems perspective. If I am struggling with a difficult piece of writing or a personal concern that needs attention, "sleeping on it" is often the best remedy. Releasing the matter from conscious thought enables me to confront it again with fresh eyes and a new point of view, to find an appropriate resolution.

God, in his infinite wisdom, provides daily, dependably, what we need. Even as He created us, God knew that our bodies would require restorative rest. He dims the glare of day and instills a nocturnal lull for ease and repose. "When you lie down, your sleep will be sweet" (Proverbs 3:24). In night's quiet pause, He offers peaceful respite from care and strain and still refreshment of body, mind, and soul. "He grants sleep to those He loves" (Psalm 127:2).

Soothing Waters

his month's calendar near my desk features the nineteenth century painting of Belgian artist George Steven's, *The Bath.* In muted tones of grayed blues and greens and the soft pastels of flesh, a lady lounges in the sanctuary of her bath. An open book perches on the folds of her discarded gown, the arm on which she leans catches up her auburn hair, sweet roses in her other hand dangle over the tub's edge, and in the soap dish lies her clock on a chain, time removed and ignored. Is there a place more evocative of serenity than the bath? Concerns are diluted in aqueous warmth, cares dissolve in rising steam.

In a lively household with three siblings, I relished the singular childhood pleasure of the bath. A little pink from a lot of sun, scented with new-mown grass and eight-o'clock air, sticky from hedge-apple battles, I sank into water which rose slowly over mulberry-painted toes. Soaking very still, fizzy skinned, I emerged pinker than before, fingers puckered, mosquito bites and rope-swing scratches a more lively red than ever.

One of the benefits of an old apartment under the eaves, which I rented as a graduate student, was a deep, claw-footed bathtub, original to the house. Unlike the modern shallow varieties which leave a bather's top half chilled, with no way to comfortably recline against awkward straight angles, the body-friendly curves of this antique tub allowed me to lie back, enveloped in soothing water to my chin. Its heavy, cast iron kept water warm for a good, long soak.

I loved the traditional European bathroom of our early marriage, its classic white tiles and commodious fixtures. The tub was wide, long, and deep, with a generous ledge on which our Kitty joined me at bath time, draping herself over the warm faucets in clouds of steaming scent, as I soaked away the frustrations of learning a foreign language, foreign money, foreign telephones, and foreign customs. Great old windows welcomed invigorating morning breezes with the fragrance of a blooming cherry tree below.

Not all parts of the world have enjoyed such liquid luxury. In some dry lands of Arabian and African peoples, cleansing was commonly waterless. An earthenware pot of burning charcoal and fragrant woods and resins was placed in a hole in the sand. Women removed their undergarments, wrapped a cloak about them to contain the fumes, and crouched over the fragrant smoke. Sweating cleansed the pores, and aromatics fumigated the lower part of the body. Then, the skin was rubbed with perfumed oils.

Rome, at its prime, was renowned for its elaborate public baths, which offered not only physical cleansing, but also spacious rooms for conversation, libraries, gardens, galleries, and shady porticos for exercise. The bather usually progressed from a cold bath, to a tepid bath, to a hot bath, followed by scrubbing with a comb and massage with aromatic oils. After another cold bath, more perfumed unguents were applied. Roman warriors returning from battle especially enjoyed bay leaves in their baths to soothe tired muscles and minds.

In the French Court of Louis XV, Madame Tallien bathed in waters scented with crushed raspberries and strawberries, followed by sponging with perfumed milk.

These luxuries sound like more time and expense than we could afford today, but the bath still seems a sanctuary, a private place for cleansing the body and renewing the spirit. David uses the images of ablution when he prays in Psalm 51:10: "Create in me a clean heart, O God; and renew a right spirit within me" (KJV). Just as a quiet soak in the bath can refresh us for the demands of living, so God's soothing waters of forgiveness can restore our soiled and flagging spirits. God sanctifies us in baptism and continues to wash us in grace to purify our souls and revive us for service. What a pleasure it is to submerge ourselves in His goodness, soak in His mercy, and bathe in His luxuriant forgiveness.

Fed by Hyacinths

After reading an enthusiastic account of perfuming winter rooms with the exquisite essence of narcissus blooms, I planted a potful, anticipating the allure of spring's early indoor arrival. But when their long-awaited aroma suffused the room, I was repelled by the acrid suggestion of burning electrical wiring. Obviously I interpret the scent differently than those who proclaim its appeal.

Undaunted in my quest to assuage stale months indoors, I tried hyacinths. Not only was my persistence rewarded with their sublime scent, but blossoms lasted for some days as their miniature bells emerged into striking flowers. Such redolent results require little effort, and it is satisfying to watch a bulb slowly develop its roots, stem, leaves, and flowers, anticipating spring.

Specially designed hyacinth vases are available, or you may use any glass with a smaller neck and larger mouth which will support the bulb above water level. The best varieties for forcing are larger bulbs designed for growing indoors. 1) Place the hyacinth bulb in the glass with its tip pointing up. 2) Fill the glass with water as close as possible to the bottom of the bulb without touching it. Sitting in water, the bulb can rot, but too far from water, the bulb can dry out. 3) Put the glass in a well-ventilated area (basement, refrigerator, garage) where temperatures stay above freezing, between 40-50 degrees. 4) Store for approximately 13 weeks, checking weekly to maintain water level. Roots will fill the glass, and a shoot will appear from the tip of the bulb. 5) When the shoot is two to three inches high, bring it into a warm room (60-70 degrees). Keep in filtered light until the shoot begins to green, then move to full sunlight. 6) The hyacinth should bloom in two to three weeks. When it begins to bloom, move it out of direct heat and sun to prolong its flowering.

Gulistan of Moslih Eddin Saadi describes the sublime pleasure of hyacinths:

"If of thy mortal goods thou art bereft,

And from thy slender store two loaves alone to thee are left,

Sell one, and with the dole

Buy hyacinths to feed the soul."

The beauty and bouquet of hyacinths must be valued indeed to trade physical food for such spiritual nourishment. Jesus used a similar metaphor when, famished in the desert heat, he rejected the devil's temptation to demonstrate his divinity by turning stones into bread. But Jesus answered, "It is written: 'Man does not live on bread alone, but on every word that comes from the mouth of God'" (Matthew 4:4).

In God's Word we find the direction for living, answers for questions, solutions for problems, comfort for concerns, solace for despair, forgiveness for sin, and the promise of eternal life. "How sweet are your words to my taste, sweeter than honey to my mouth!" (Psalms 119:103). Shouldn't such savory sustenance be a staple in our diet?

My Darling Clementines

*D*uring the winter season when little out-of-doors is perfuming the air, or, at least, we are less often in our yards and gardens to enjoy winter's own essences, clementines, tantalizing miniature orange citrus fruits, are a particular pleasure. Aromatic, free of troublesome seeds, easy to peel, they are just the right size for taking the edge off an impatient appetite. I like them at room temperature to bring out their succulent taste, savoring their bursting, sweet tartness, slowly, not to miss one fragment of fragrant pulp. Peeling clementines scents the hands with their vivid oil and provides a simple salad or a refreshing dessert.

But the eating is not the extent of clementines' pleasures. Atop my refrigerator, trays of their scented peels dry in a matter of days for use in potpourri, which can be enjoyed all year. Orange and tangerine peels can be preserved in the same manner.

Making potpourri, an ancient art, reminds me of the word's connotation of "an incongruous combination." The word could describe most of us in our ambiguities. Perhaps we are both a fun-loving friend and a disciplined employee, a sun-seeking gardener and a fireside bibliophile, a talented cook but hopeless with computers, an eager traveler who can't read a map, a painstaking artist but an impatient shopper. We are each a mixture of faults and foibles, talents and abilities. Our qualities don't always seem to complement one another. But we can design the personal potpourri that is our self. God will help us eliminate the unkind elements, the distasteful qualities, the weak traces in our Christian living, so that we may lead balanced, pleasing lives, which demonstrate His hand in our creation.

The composition may be as complicated or as simple as you like, but a potpourri made of fresh ingredients to your individual taste will certainly be more appealing than the artificially scented wood-chip variety commonly available.

If you enjoy gardening, save some of your favorite dried blossoms—jonquil, lavender, rose, carnation, iris, peony, pinks, hydrangea, or experiment with others you favor. Add some of your dried garden herbs—lemon verbena, mint, thyme, rosemary, bay. Include any dried roots, berries, seeds, pods, or fruits which you find attractive. Whole nutmeg, allspice, and cinnamon bark will contribute a pleasant spiciness. Fixatives, like orris root and oakmoss, available from botanical suppliers, will keep the fragrance from fading. To create a beautiful potpourri, consider the colors of your ingredients, and save a few of the prettiest blossoms for the top.

Be sure all ingredients are bone dry, as any moisture will encourage mold to ruin your blend. Place them in a large paper bag. Add a few drops of natural essential oil to complement the fragrant components you have selected. (Additional oil may be added later to revive scent as it fades.) Then gently mix and allow to cure for about a month in a cool, dark place, gently stirring every few days. (Be careful that oils which may seep through the bag cannot damage anything touching it.)

A combination I have recently created includes the following dried ingredients: thyme twigs, rosemary leaves, and tarragon blossoms from the garden; balsam snippings from a discarded Christmas wreath; orange and clementine peel; allspice berries; a little ground coriander; with 1 part carnation oil to 2 parts vanilla oil. Making potpourri is not a science. These were simply gleanings I had available and scents I like. The result is surprising and lovely.

Try your own preferences and whatever you have on hand. When the potpourri is ready, display your creation in a beautiful bowl, perhaps one with special personal meaning, to delight your family and guests. May it remind you to thank God for your life's fragrant complexity and to ask Him to help you with its continued refinement.

Spicy Company

When the weather turns cooler and evenings become longer, making pomanders can bring family or friends together around the kitchen table. Once ingredients are assembled, you can enjoy a leisurely evening actually conversing, savoring the close proximity of one another's company. This is an engaging activity for older children and adults, which can contribute to those shared moments for which we seldom find time when the television is blaring or family members are racing off to separate events.

The word "pomander" comes from the French "pomme d'ambre," meaning "apple of amber." The ball-shaped aggregation of herbs and spices looked like an apple, and its primary fixative was ambergris (from the intestines of whales). Perfumes and fragrant materials were blended, then added to a cohesive ball of beeswax or plain soil to create various aromatic pomanders. Later these evolved into beautiful metalwork and jeweled ornaments.

Aristocratic ladies and gentlemen originally wore these pomanders on a ribbon or chain around the neck or at the belt as protection against odor, infection, and bad luck. They were held to the nose to prevent smelling the stench or contracting disease from rotting garbage, open sewers, and the general unsanitary conditions of medieval streets and their wretches.

Today's spiced fruit pomanders are easier to make than originally. They impart a delightful aroma to closets, drawers, chests, and as an added benefit, keep moths away.

Directions:

Select a ripe apple (a small one for your first effort). You may also use grapefruit, lemons, limes, pears, or thin-skinned oranges. All should be sound and firm without bruises or soft spots. Holding the fruit gently, cover its entire surface by poking the cloves' pointed ends into the fruit's skin. A small fruit will require approximately two to three cans of cloves. (When using citrus fruit, it may be necessary to prick holes with an ice pick and place whole cloves into these holes. I have found apples and pears less time consuming). Finish inserting whole cloves into your foundation fruit in one sitting. Overnight drying lessons the quality of the pomander, as the fruit will begin to deteriorate.

Create one of the following spice mixtures, or one of your own, equaling 2 Tablespoons:

1. 3 teaspoons cinnamon + 1 teaspoon each ground cloves, ginger, and nutmeg
2. 3 teaspoons cinnamon + 2 teaspoons cardamom + 1 teaspoon allspice
3. 1 teaspoon each ground sassafras, ginger, anise, fennel, cinnamon, and cardamom (a nostalgic candy scent)

Mix any one of the above spice recipes with 8 Tablespoons orris root (available from a botanical supply resource or pharmacy). In these mixtures, spices reduce shrinkage, and the orris root acts as a fixative to make the fragrance last longer.

In a bowl, roll the clove-studded fruit with your mixture of spices and orris root daily for ten to fourteen days, turning the pomander in the mixture. The dry mixture should evenly coat the fruit.

After the ball has been rolled in your mixture of spices and orris root, wrap it in newspaper, place in a drawer or closet, and let the fruit dry out for four to six weeks. Save your spice mixture for another pomander.

When the fruit has dried, gently shake, tap, or lightly brush off excess spice mixture. Add this excess to your left-over spice mixture to use again.

The pomander is now ready to hang in a bag of fine net or to be tied in ribbons, and should stay fragrant for years to come. Older children can make these as Christmas gifts for teachers. Add mistletoe to create a Christmas ornament for hanging in a doorway.

If the family is helping, try making a bowlful. Or begin a bowl and add to it through the year, or annually during the holiday season.

Each time you smell the spicy pomander, you will remember how God spices your life with the company of family and friends with whom you made these enduring scented reminders.

Creature Comfort

*C*ontrasted with dogs, who need a helping hand with bathing, cats are fastidious creatures. Although the antibacterial substance in cats' saliva is not strong enough to prevent infection, it keeps their groomed fur smelling fresh. After being petted, a cat often washes its fur to get rid of human odors, or to further its association by tasting a companion's scent.

Our timid indoor/outdoor charmer, Waifur, is named for her disheveled, forsaken appearance when she claimed our affections. Also known as The Divine Miss Debris, she drags in all manner of soil and rubbish, calling to mind James Thurber's description of a fine Burgundy: "It's a naive domestic . . . without any breeding, but I think you will be amused by its presumption." A mobile room freshener, she trails spicy currents in her auburn fur from a nap beneath the bay bush. Cats also act as pollinators, transporting pollen on their whiskers, faces, and fur. They similarly pollinate our lives with the blessing they bear us.

Just after our marriage in Kansas, we acquired our beloved white Kitty, namesake of *Gunsmoke's* big-hearted Dodge City character. She traveled with us back and forth to Europe, banging along baggage conveyers without complaint. She was a constant and comforting presence in changing surroundings. Kitty joined me on the floor for morning exercises, or waited for Michael on a mat outside the shower. She spent her days sprawled on the warm ledge over a radiator, watching sheep herded beyond our window, or snoozed in her favorite chair in a sunbeam. In the evenings she slept on our shoes until the very climax of a video movie, when she wanted to be fed, then joined us in bed for a warm snuggle. On one rare occasion, when we took Kitty outdoors into the lawn, a young boy reached to pet her irresistible white fur. "She looks just like a cloud," he sighed.

After nearly twenty years of her fond companionship, Kitty became increasingly weak and disinterested in food. Finally, she lost her appetite altogether, a sure sign of her failing in that she loved to eat. At last she withdrew to quiet spots for long rests, although her eyes often were not closed, so she was not sleeping well either. It became painfully obvious that it was time to allow her to go and that she was ready. The night before we took her in, Michael let her spend a long while out-of-doors, resting with him in our swing.

By morning, she was hardly able to walk. We spent the next morning with her until her appointment. "It is time to go to heaven," I told her as I lifted her little frame, which had become a frail shadow of her twenty-pound prime. "And you won't have to take a plane to get there," Michael assured her, in reference to all her travels with us to and from Europe. Her little mews en route had none of her old vigor. Our veterinarian, a most compassionate man, allowed us to hold and stroke her until she passed peacefully away. Gently, he wrapped her favorite towel about her.

At home, we gave her her old stuffed mouse, which she had loved to dunk in her milk bowl, and placed her in the backyard grave that Michael had dug in preparation. Michael read a little prayer, which I had written for her but was unable to read, then buried her. Just as he finished, we looked up at the sky. A puffy, white cloud floated overhead.

The brief lives of our pets are long on blessing. We owe to them our loving attention, and to God our gratitude.

"How many are your works, O Lord! In wisdom you made them all; the earth is full of your creatures" (Psalm 104:24).

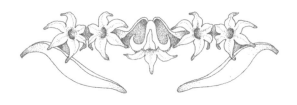

Vanilla Splendor

*V*anilla is one of my favorite fragrances for winter, a mellow complement to a mesmerizing fire. On window sills, kitchen counters, living room tables, vanilla candles imbue a room with a warm and inviting aura. Vanilla's luscious fragrance also makes a soothing tea. Simply split and open the bean, chop it into small pieces, and add to loose black tea, allowing the tea to absorb the vanilla flavor for several weeks. Brew the tea with vanilla pieces as usual for an indulgently aromatic cup.

The vanilla orchid climbs tall trees of tropical forests, reaching for warmth of the sun to bloom its fragrant, waxy flowers. In the vanilla orchid's native Mexico, tiny bees pollinate the plants. Elsewhere, a small citrus thorn is used to pollinate the orchids by hand just as they blossom. When this delicate procedure is successful, bunches of beans ripen up to eight months on the vine and are picked at the perfect stage of yellow firmness. At the high prices beans command, growers deter thieves by stamping their beans with pins in a distinctive pattern, which remains visible even after curing. Some vanilla farmers have watch dogs patrolling family plots.

After being sorted by size, vanilla beans are steeped in very hot water to stop organic changes and prevent them from splitting open. As beans sweat in canvas-lined boxes, they become darker and develop their rich aroma. Then, to discourage mold, beans are spread on sacking in the sun to dry for approximately ten days, in a ventilated room for about two months, and in curing trunks for a few months more. When seed pods are harvested and cured carefully, crystals form, frosting the outside of the wrinkled bean.

Like aged wine and moldy cheese, which grow more delicious with time, vanilla beans develop their value slowly, as they are cured. An analogy may be drawn between the maturing of vanilla beans and our own aging. Growing older can mean carefully selecting and tending our best spiritual qualities to develop them, through the years, to their fullest potential.

It can be difficult, however, to reconcile this perspective with our culture's aversion to age. We try to respect the elderly, but we tend to shun their company. We attempt to keep up with the most current trends. We camouflage the wrinkles, color the gray, cinch the sags. We worry about financial security, about incapacitating illness and pain, about losing spontaneity, about declining mental acuity, and about who will care for us.

But God reminds us that our escapism and fears are unnecessary. "The glory of young men is their strength, gray hair the splendor of the old," advises Proverbs 20:29. While our vitality may be diminished with age, our splendor is not? I wonder at these words. If splendor is luster and brilliance, I certainly see less of it in my skin and memory.

This Scripture is not referring to our preoccupation with physical vitality, however, but rather to spiritual glory.

As my father entered his nineties, I remarked with gratitude on his health and vigor. He still roto-tilled his vegetable garden in his signature long-sleeved white shirt and tie. He sustained lively conversation on current events. But this Proverb seems to suggest that what is more worthy than such admirable hardiness is the patient equanimity he has always exemplified and which he continues to display despite suffering a debilitating stroke. Even when health and circumstances are impaired with the accumulation of years, what shines in those who endure with grace is often their even-tempered composure, their calm acceptance of restrictions, their non-judgmental response to others, their persistent hopefulness. Such is the splendor of age to wish we might aspire.

Present Tense

*T*he great oak table stretched to its fullest length with every available leaf. A smaller children's table sat at its end. Table cloths reserved for special occasions were retrieved and spread, dinnerware distributed. The aroma of Thanksgiving turkey and pumpkin pie permeated the house. Stomachs gurgled. Children circled their aproned mothers and aunts in the kitchen, hoping for a hint that dinner would soon be ready. Oh, it was hard to wait!

In our escalated impatience, today we stand in front of a microwave oven and wish it would hurry. We speed around drivers adhering to the speed limit. Our blood pressure begins to rise when only a few customers precede us in line. We acquire debt so that we can have merchandise now.

Waiting seems increasingly difficult. When my father was a young man, his generation generally accepted the necessity of waiting for the pleasures of later satisfaction. Depravations of the Depression, service in the military, battling back to health after being wounded in World War II meant waiting to marry, to build a home, to start a family, to establish himself in business. Others did the same.

Lessons in patience seem lost on us today. We insist on immediate gratification, often relinquishing more worthy goals in the process. Merchants make it easy to indulge our whims by offering easy credit. We slake our current desires and move on to the next before distinguishing between needs and wants or before evaluating our motivations, expectations, goals, and values. In a frenzy for novelty, we want what is most current as quickly as possible, although today's interests will be forgotten tomorrow. Depth and duration depreciate. We chafe at delay.

We need to be reminded that to appreciate life we must be there, not racing through it, anticipating what is next. What is the hurry? Can we delay death or hasten heaven? Speedy satisfactions prompt us to demand our own way, to become irritated by circumstances beyond our control and by people who impede our ambitions.

Scripture frequently emphasizes the virtue of patience: "Be completely humble and gentle; be patient, bearing with one another" (Ephesians 4:2). "Therefore, as God's chosen people, holy and dearly loved, clothe yourselves with compassion, kindness, humility, gentleness and patience" (Colossians 3:12). By learning to wait, we become more conscious of the needs of others, we recognize that there may not be an immediate solution to every problem, we focus on the present, we sort out what truly matters, and we relinquish control to God, who measures time by eternity.

Breakfast Blessing

I love breakfast time—the fresh, clean slate of day on which anything might be written; the rich aroma of brewing coffee; of toast smeared with butter and zesty marmalade; of simmering oatmeal and raisins. Eschewing the too-perky commentary of radio and television commentators and blaring commercial interruptions, I relish the quiet interlude with my own thoughts and the early, inky paper.

The risen Christ made breakfast for his disciples early one morning near the Sea of Tiberias. As the fishermen approached the shore, weary from fishing all night without a catch, Jesus directed them where to cast their nets. When they followed His instructions, their nets were filled with so many fish, they struggled to haul them in. Jesus knew they would certainly be hungry. The scent of grilled fish and baked bread likely accompanied His invitation to his disciples. "Jesus said to them, 'Come and have breakfast'" (John 21:12).

This simple story is beautifully reassuring, its lesson clear. Beginning the morning in the presence of our Lord can provide us with the direction we need to make the day productive and satisfying. A short prayer, meditation, or Bible reading can offer divine advice for the day ahead, bless our endeavors, and nourish our souls.

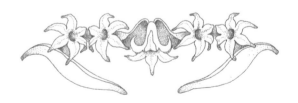

Grime of the Heart

*I*n a rich rush from beans to brewing, the roasty aroma of coffee seems to widen the eyes, stimulate the digestive juices, and perk up the lingering languor of night. The ritual of preparing the percolator or coffee-maker propels us through those mindless early moments and generates anticipation of the day ahead.

Unfortunately, a dirty little secret can lurk in the making of that satisfying cup. While filling the coffee-maker one recent morning, I caught sight of a dark shadow through the louvered lid. When I peeled back the top, not exactly designed for easy removal, I found disgusting black patches in nooks and corners of the reservoir. What was growing in there? Mold? Mildew? I didn't want to know. The nastiness had developed in spite of running regular cycles of vinegar through the unit, as the manufacturer had directed. I began to consider other coffee-makers, less maintained, in offices, restaurants. What might be multiplying in the dark recesses of those machines that coffee drinkers don't know?

Our hidden sins are often like that coffee-maker grime. No one may know about them. We do our best to obscure them, even from ourselves. But the covetousness, selfishness, greed, and pride settled in our souls grow unobserved to contaminate the spiritual cups we pour forth. Our actions may appear desirable, but who knows our motivations and prejudices? Even a dose of occasional religion cannot eradicate persistent impurities. Those sins require a regular scrubbing, distasteful as it may be. This means examining ourselves honestly, repenting of those sins we try so hard to conceal, seeking forgiveness, and becoming vigilant for signs of recurrence. David's prayer is fitting: "Forgive my hidden faults. . . . May the words of my mouth and the meditation of my heart be pleasing in your sight, O Lord, my Rock and my Redeemer" (Psalm 19:12, 14). Cleansed with God's promise of forgiveness, we are reassured that we can once again offer cups of blessing.

Cooking Smells

*I*n the early evenings of childhood, supper smells from next-door kitchens wafted throughout the neighborhood. We could tell who would find fried chicken or apple pie on their dinner menus, or who might be subject to liver and onions. Windows tended to be open, moms were often home to cook, families ate together at an established hour, and eating out was still reserved for special occasions.

Neighbors visited in one-another's yards, helped each other with projects, and interacted in neighboring lives. One of our neighbors simply shouted a "Yoo-Hoo!" through the screen door and let herself in. And at the nearby market, we regularly met others in the vicinity.

Foreign visitors to our suburban neighborhoods today often remark about how isolated residents appear to be. We live behind the closed windows of climate-controlled houses and spend considerable time in the confines of our cars, taking us to distant jobs, shopping, and entertainment. We may be acquainted with only a handful of those who live on our street.

Perhaps it is natural that as communities become more populated, relationships between members become less intimate. Feeling too close for comfort, we become sensitive to infringement on our space. We prefer to keep our distance.

And our country's sense of independence is fiercely ingrained. We think of our nation's founding by individualists who struck out on their own against the unfamiliar and dangerous to forge new lives for themselves. The history of westward expansion, at least in legend, is one of rugged individualism. We imagine explorers, pioneers, cowboys as self-sufficient, and it is true that they often had to rely on their own resourcefulness, intuition, and intellect. But accounts of their survival and success do not always allude to the support of others on whom they relied for help building a home, rounding up stray livestock, or fighting a prairie fire. Frontier communities began only with the integrated commitment of many residents.

When individualism is carried to the extreme, we have little use for each other. We see others as nuisances, impediments to our own objectives. We tend to ignore our responsibilities to relationships with others in our family, community, and world.

What can we do to instill in a child a sense of his place in the world, of his commitment to others? We might begin back at the family dinner table. Gathered with loved ones, here a child learns to identify him or herself as a participant in family matters. As the issues of parents or siblings are aired and exchanged, a child becomes informed of, interested in, and respectful of the activities and ideas of other family members. Through parental comment, approval, disapproval, and advice, a youngster gains moral compass. The child learns mannered and appropriate consideration. Setting the table, taking out trash, chores involved in mealtime ritual teach children the importance of everyone's contribution to the household, to the welfare of a unit larger than self. Such vital guidance and education seldom occur when individual family members eat on the run at varying times or watch separate television programs in different rooms.

In recent decades, misguided parents and teachers have promoted children's self-esteem by unconditional praise, whether merited by behavior or not. When children feel they are beyond improvement, is it any wonder that they disdain the direction of authority? When a sense of self has become inflated, is it any surprise that the concerns or feelings of others are trampled? When ego is emphasized, is it any mystery why relationships suffer?

Children do, in fact, need to be encouraged in their efforts to gain confidence that they can face the challenges which they will confront. But they learn this by established expectations, praise for accomplishment, guidance when an effort has failed, and personal example, not by instilling unmerited pride. Children need to know, rather, that modesty, empathy, and thoughtfulness are desirable virtues, that the welfare of others matters. They need to be reminded of Jesus' admonishment in Matthew 22:39: "Love your neighbor as yourself." By enacting these words, they will become successful and happy in their relationships, responsible in their communities.

Whether learning to read or swim or play piano, children need guidance and practice to gain facility. How much more do children need disciplined training in moral virtue. Lessons learned while eating with family can reinforce even children's smallest efforts to develop a generous spirit, like not taking the last piece of liver.

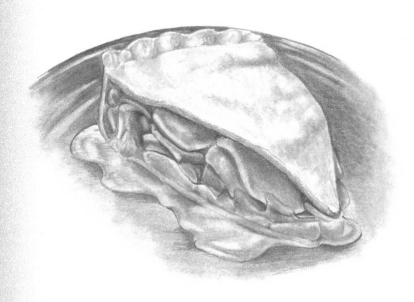

Fine Wine

*I*n early summer, we children would join Mother's slow cruise of rural Kansas roads, noting locations of sprawling shrubs with large white umbrella-shaped blossoms. Later in the season we retraced our trip to the same bushes, now heavy and drooping with clusters of ripe elderberries. Unconcerned with traffic on such quiet lanes, Mother would stop the old station wagon, children clambering out, through ditches, baskets and buckets in hand, to collect the juicy, purplish-black berries. From the bitter berries, she made a delicious, dark, disappearing jelly, which my father especially relished on buttered bread as a simple dessert.

My uncle had other uses for the sumptuous berries. Decent into his basement met the pungent, musty smell of crushed elderberries and grapes foaming in crocks. After fermenting, juice was strained from pulp and transferred to wooden kegs with sugar and water. Copper tubing inserted into the keg's cork was bent into a glass of water to monitor bubbles as the juice became wine. When bubbles no longer appeared, the wine was sealed in jugs with wax. Samples of the finished product, passed around in a fog of cigar smoke at Christmas time, were duly praised by admiring brothers. A sip, in my youthful estimation, was sufficient, a waste of precious jam potential.

John 2:1-11 recounts Jesus' first miracle, turning water into wine. While attending a wedding celebration, Jesus' mother remarked to her son that the wine had run out. In spite of His response that His time had not yet come, Mary told His disciples to be prepared to follow Jesus' directions. Jesus later asked His followers to fill stone jars with water, then draw it out for the host, who was impressed with the fine quality of the wine into which the water had been transformed.

The story demonstrates valuable lessons concerning prayer. To begin with, Mary was not specific about the solution she preferred to the problem, nor was she insistent. She did not tell Jesus what should be done, nor did she repeat her concern. She simply brought the matter before Him and allowed Him to find His own manner and moment to respond. In asking the disciples to prepare to receive direction, she had faith that her supplication would not be ignored. Then Mary waited patiently for Jesus to act. She could not have anticipated the miraculous way in which Jesus would provide, or the wonderful taste of His provision.

Mary's approach is a worthy model for our own prayers. Often we bear our petitions with preconceptions about how we want God to respond, imagining we know what remedy is best. We may belabor the request by repeated demands for speedy resolution. Sometimes we are not entirely sure our prayers are heard, so we take matters into our own impatient hands. And too often, we use prayer only as a last resort when we have first attempted every other human avenue, and our own inadequate or misguided efforts have failed.

Imagine being able to talk as intimately to Jesus as Mary did when she was in the same room with Him. But we can, and this is the wonder! At any time, in any place or circumstance, we can speak directly to the One who created and sustains all that exists. Try to reach the President of the United States, or the state governor, the mayor, your physician, or even an appliance repairman. God never requires us to push a series of buttons at the tone, or leave a message, or remain on hold. He is always there, already informed about our concern, and eager to help.

We don't need to use "thee" and "thou," or fold our hands, or even close our eyes. Prayer can be simply a spoken or silent expression of what is on our minds at the moment, while making toast, tying a shoelace, shampooing hair, or standing in line.

In His way and time, God may respond by suggesting a viable means of helping ourselves. On other occasions, He can answer our prayers with a rich and surprising generosity that we are incapable of imagining. To savor His superlative wine, we must consult God often, believe He will answer, and submit to His will. Then prepare to be drink of His delicious exuberance, and thank God for His blessing.

The miracles with which God answers our prayers should come as no surprise to us, for we see evidence of His wonders all about us in His world. Which is more amazing: that Jesus could turn water into wine or that He can turn rain into elderberries?

Bread of Life

When pioneers crossed dry expanses on their way west, landscape lost its verdure, wheels of wagons shrank and wobbled, skin parched, their sense of distance warped. But in the salty residue of dried lake beds, they often found saleratus (sodium or potassium bicarbonate) to leaven bread, which sustained them on their long journey.

Is there a smell more wholesome than baking loaves of beautiful brown bread? Regardless how far a baker may be from the apron-lapped, nose-dusted image, the irresistible aroma of rising bread prompts us to thank God for His providence.

Bread is a blessed gift, truly. We marvel at the mystery of rising bread, wheat and yeast, liquid and shortening transformed to delicious and nutritious heights. Even greater is the wonder of the risen Christ, who became man, died, and rose from the grave so that we also may have abundant life. This baby from Bethlehem, a town meaning "house of bread," came as living food to satisfy our deepest hunger.

Bread is not only the staff of our physical life, but of our spiritual life as well. Jesus said, "I am the living bread that came down from heaven. If anyone eats of this bread, he will live forever. This bread is my flesh, which I will give for the life of the world" (John 6:51). "Whoever eats my flesh and drinks my blood has eternal life, and I will raise him up at the last day" (John 6:54).

Jesus instituted the Lord's Supper, wherein bread is broken and wine poured forth, to remind us that He gave His body and blood to atone for our sins. In this sacred rite, God forgives our failings and affirms that by faith we will commune again with Him in the hereafter. We thank Him for this life-giving gift, which sustains us on our journey heavenward.

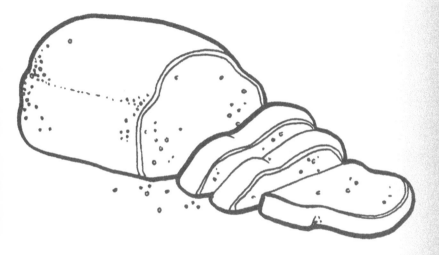

Radiant Fire

he smell of smoke kindled fear in the hearts of early pioneers on the plains. From late summer throughout the fall, tall prairie grasses parched by summer heat and drought were easily ignited by a spark from lightening, a campfire, or a passing train. Once lit, fires swept relentlessly across vast landscapes, threatening homesteads in their path. The glare of red skies kept families awake, scanning the horizon to monitor shifts in wind and the creeping progress of blazes. Even plowed ground around property and neighboring waterways could not always secure homes and fields from flames, which jumped these guards in blowing weeds or grass. Faces blackened, eyes stinging, frontier families battled blazes and clouds of acrid smoke with pails of water and dirt, wet blankets, grain sacks, and even petticoats.

Despite its destructive power, fire on the prairie was also used to advantage. Before the arrival of pioneers, aboriginal plainsmen set fire to grassland to drive bison over cliffs, where they harvested meat, skins, bones, organs, and other useful parts for food, clothing, shelter, weapons, tools, and utensils. And, because numerous dialects made communication difficult between tribes, and sometimes even between families, fire was a means of universal communication via smoke signals.

Today, ranchers deliberately set and control spring prairie fires to aerate roots and encourage new growth, and to eliminate invasive shrubs and small trees which hamper the grazing of livestock. Travelers on highways which intersect Midwest pastures may still smell the sharp fumes of burning grassland or be caught in a dense fog of smoke if winds shift unexpectedly.

Fire is used often in the Bible as a symbol of God's presence. God appeared in a burning bush to call Moses to lead His people out of bondage (Exodus 3:2-4), then led His people by a pillar of fire to the promised land (Exodus 13:21). The Holy Spirit descended on His apostles with tongues of fire at Pentecost (Acts 2:3).

God will also use fire to wreak His vengeance on those who reject Him, as Isaiah 5:24 describes: "Therefore, as tongues of fire lick up straw and as dry grass sinks down in the flames, so their roots will decay and their flowers blow away like dust; for they have rejected the law of the Lord Almighty and spurned the word of the Holy One of Israel."

Preaching such heavy-handed "fire and brimstone" messages has fallen out of favor today. Our discomfort in being reminded of the seriousness of our transgressions and the gravity of their consequences does little to promote church attendance. Few of us are willing to accept blame or claim fault. Attempting to justify our behavior with handy excuses, we blame upbringing, environment, or circumstances, but ignore personal accountability. We prefer to disregard the duty and responsibility we have to obey God's commandments. But only when we recognize our sin and failure and understand that, humanly, we can never perfectly follow God's will, can we see our need for His exuberant forgiveness. Once we realize that our efforts to earn heaven will never be good enough, and accept that only Christ's perfect life and death can atone for our imperfection, we feel relief. Assured of our salvation, we can relinquish the burden of good behavior and replace it with a cheerful desire to love. Although as humans, our commitment to living rightly will need daily renewal, as redeemed, we may fearlessly approach judgment. "For he has rescued us form the dominion of darkness and brought us into the kingdom of the Son he loves, in whom we have redemption, the forgiveness of sins" (Colossians 1:13-14).

There is both terror and benefit in fire. Burning on the plains can be fearsome in its destruction of wanton growth, but it also promises grass will return, revived and renewed. Similarly, when fire accompanies God's return, it will purge the earth, destroying evil and the unbelieving, but offering radiant glory to those who accept His promises.

Ship of Fools

A broiling summer day could mean inviting a sister or cousin, or the dog, for cooling in the creek.

Through scratchy brush, down muddy banks, we approached the earthy richness and placid splashing which drew us to a place apart. The dog, always a German Shepherd variation of Rick or Mick, plunged ahead or joined us for a swim until his nose ferreted out the smell of fun afield. Some afternoons we simply sat folding lawn chairs in a ripple, dangling our feet while engrossed in a book. Other times we took the little row boat on a laughable jaunt.

Devoid of navigational skill, we bumped a rotting carcass on a slimy bank, evaded a water snake, or brushed a nest of spiders in an overhanging branch, shrieking in revulsion and paddling wildly to extract ourselves. For short stretches, the stream carried us through intermittent light and shadow. When the dog found us again, he attempted to join the hilarity in the boat, throwing his muddy paws over the side for a boost, then tipping the boat precariously as he circled, shook, and stank. Blushed with sun, smeared with mud, smelling of sweat and suntan lotion, passengers frequently disembarked to carry the bark over rocky low points. We never managed to venture too far since retracing our travails upstream usually took twice the time of our downstream trip.

Excursions in our little boat bring to mind the Sunday school picture of Jesus standing in the fishing boat of his quavering disciples, raising his arms to quiet the storm (Matthew 8:23-27). Here He miraculously intervened to subdue the sea and rescue His followers. More often, however, God gives us instead the ability to solve our own problems, to avoid entangling predicaments, steer clear of dangerous temptations, and avoid the reeking carcasses of everyday difficulties, occasioned by our foolish impertinence. Sometime challenges seem more substantial, but even then, He gives us the strength to pick up our own boat and carry it over the shoals and shallows. Working within us, He helps us arrive at our own solutions to restore broken relationships, overcome selfishness, conquer fear, or relieve pain which may have stalled or imperiled us.

Our prayers are seldom answered by immediate or breathtaking miracles, but usually by the evolving discovery of a feasible approach or a new perspective. If we listen closely, we can hear His steady oars as they splash behind us, the captain of our ship navigating and propelling us through life's waters.   "May the Lord direct your hearts into God's love and Christ's perseverance" (II Thessalonians 3:5).

Coming Clean

*W*hen we think of the fragrance industry, we usually imagine experienced "noses" creating the seductive perfumes we find beautifully packaged in enticing bottles. In fact, a greater part of fragrance development is devoted to the scents we find in everyday products like air freshener, bathroom tissue, furniture polish, and especially cleaning agents. The fresh scents of dish detergents, soaps, shampoos, household cleansers, and laundry powders are designed to provoke clean and sanitary associations. If detergents smell good, we tend to believe they are effective.

Because water for washing was scarce in the desert, wealthy ancients in dry lands often fumigated their bedding and clothing over braziers of burning aromatics. Still today we practice the old custom of placing small bags of scent between garments and linens when we tuck lavender sachets into our drawers and closets. Some country laundresses sun their wash on fragrant shrubs. Lavender water may be made by boiling lavender in distilled water, cooling, and straining, for use in the rinse cycle or steam iron.

Clean laundry always give me a sense of satisfaction in the neat, softly scented stack of towels, freshly pressed shirts and blouses, drawers filled once more with clean socks and underwear, sunny sheets redolent of lawn. When I reflect on childhood memories of my mother's activities, her days seem inundated in laundry. From a hallway laundry chute, daily piles of dirty clothes from a six-member family accumulated with what must have seemed to my mother astonishing rapidity. I see her making endless trips to the basement, sorting mounds and mounds of wash, pouring her magic cleaning potions into steaming tubs—bluing, bleaches, boosters, detergents, a symphony of sudsy smells. Carrying load after load to the backyard, pins in her mouth, she hung line after line. We liked to bury our faces in the flying freshness of her carefully whitened sheets. She followed more trips to the back yard to retrieve dried laundry, snapping out wrinkles in stacks and stacks of folding.

Before steam irons and easy-care fabrics, Mother dampened clothes with a sprinkle of water from a flick of the wrist, rolled them, and set them aside to moisten. She stiffened my father's collars and cuffs by dipping them in a solution of powdered starch dissolved in boiling water. Although her ironing basket must have felt bottomless to her, watching her iron lent me a certain peace. Her measured motions followed a rhythmic pattern for shirts and skirts. The swoosh of steam, smell of starch, and repeated thump of the padded board created a quiet time to talk, to ask questions, or to listen. Today I appreciate my own ironing for its same slow pace, a placid interlude for contemplation. The time spent seems a small gift to my husband to send him into the world presentably. An acquaintance once confided that she was not about to iron the tails of her husband's shirts because they wouldn't show anyway. Her comment prompted me to consider how stingy we often are in even our smallest demonstrations of affection.

The scent of laundry hanging to dry reminds me that even as we trudge daily into the world to be soiled and to sin again, we always begin renewed and refreshed by the clean apparel of forgiveness with which God clothes us. He scrubs away our most tenacious grime in the blood of His Son, airs our souls in the pure wind of the Spirit, and smoothes the wrinkles of our wrongdoing to make us respectable once more. Daily we pray the words of Psalm 51:2: "Wash me thoroughly from my iniquity and cleanse me from my sin" (KJV). In I John 1:9 we find assurance of God's forgiving response: "If we confess our sins, he is faithful and just to forgive us our sins, and to cleanse us from all unrighteousness" (KJV). Freshly absolved, we can billow sweetly in the sunshine of God's grace.

Clove Encounters

*C*limbing to the dentist office with fear and trembling, we were met on the narrow stairs by the smell of clove. Adrenaline surged, heightening our nervousness. Before fluoride, we would surely require fillings. I always hoped to be first of the children, to avoid the slow dread of the waiting room. The suspended view of the street below, the austerity of the dentist's high-necked white coat and demeanor, his whispered consultation with Mother, the glaring light, the sting of the needle, the whir of the drill, the swishing and spitting, my grip on the chair's arm, the small consolation of pencils after—all are infused in my memory by the smell of clove.

Fortunately, the scent of clove acquired more pleasant associations over time.

I discovered the sharp sweetness of clove chewing gum in its orange wrapper. Carnations were a favorite inexpensive flower for birthday bouquets or corsage occasions. And the spicy clove of Bath's pinks and stock have come to rank among my favorite floral fragrances.

In retrospect, even the clove of the dentist office could be cast in a positive light, in its ministrations to our oral health. The scent of clove oil no longer permeates dental offices as it once did when analgesics were mixed by hand. But dentists still use eugenol, the anesthetic and pharmaceutical germicide from the oil of clove buds, to soothe the discomfort of nerve pain and prevent infection.

When our own nerves have become traumatized from physical, emotional, or spiritual pain, when we feel sensitive to every minor assault on our tolerance, God relieves our distress by reassuring us of his comforting nearness. When we suffer from the shrill whine of daily stress, when persistent demands bore through our consciousness, when our muscles clench under strain, when the pleasant rewards of life seem far from sufficient, we need a close encounter with our Lord.

Sometimes the attacks on our well-being are so debilitating that we feel out of God's reach. Neither palliatives nor platitudes can console us. God seems distant, prayer is a struggle, and we don't even know what to say. At our most desperate, desolate, and disconsolate, when all we can manage is a cry of distress, God knows our need. His dependable presence calms our tension; His compassionate voice assuages our anguish; His gentle touch salves our hurt. He leans close to us and breathes His consoling words, "For I am the Lord, your God, who takes hold of your right hand and says to you, 'Do not fear; I will help you'" (Isaiah 41:13).

Permanent Solution

Always among the most immediate demands of relocating, right after finding a church, grocery store, physician, bank, and library, is the search for a new hairdresser. This trivial, vain concern is precipitated by a long history of hair horrors. Along with a book to read, I have learned to carry a grocery bag as a cover-up for the too frequent dreadful do. My earliest approach in a new community was asking for stylist recommendations from other women, any women—the lady who registered the car tag, the coffee shop waitress, the filling station clerk, the bank teller, the laundromat attendant. I discovered that this was not the most productive method of locating a hairdresser by their answers to "Who does your hair?" Some responses have included, "Mom." "I used to go to a nice girl who just quit to begin welding school." "I trade my neighbor turnips for a trim." "If I ask him when he is in the right mood, my husband will snip the ends." "There's a good salon nearby. You get to try a new stylist every visit." "Hairdresser? I've worn my hair this way for years."

Sans reliable recommendations, I finally decided to approach the quest logically and reasonably, as I might shop for a mattress or a refrigerator. I would research what was available and try to find a salon to meet my requirements, which did not seem so demanding: knowledge, experience, personal concern. From yellow page listings, I eliminated ads with artsy illustrations of aeronautically engineered coiffures, cute names like Lucy Doo's or Margie's Manes. I also skipped over ads in which tanning was in boldest type, and I avoided the "children welcome" ads. Armed with a list of promising possibilities and a street map, I spotted the first salon.

Rather than a stop, it became a drive-by. Neon lights pulsated from the window.

I tried a salon down the street. I was happy to find it busy, often a good sign, and providing me an opportunity to observe the operation first hand. The only women not on canes were being helped to hobble from sink to dryer. Silver and blue were popular tints.

Around the block and around the block, I finally located the next obscure address in a vacant office building. There I found two unoccupied young ladies staring at my unexpected entrance as though a customer were a rare, intrusive oddity.

At the next beauty parlor, a boy who hardly looked old enough to drive was assigned to me. "You must have a lot of experience," I led. "Oh yes, he replied, I've been doing hair for two months now."

The final salon on my list resembled a high-tech funeral parlor, stylists in floaty black choir robes, black walls, pin-points of light, which did not assure me that it was in the client's interest to see what was happening to her hair.

Heading home, disappointed at my fruitless, well-organized efforts, I caught sight of another little shop. Here the assigned stylist asked about the history of my hair, listened to my desires, offered recommendations, explained a healthful approach, and snipped small swatches from my hair to analyze. "We promise to take good care of your hair," she chirped. I felt comfortable at last and believed her promise.

Efforts to deal with my problem hair began before I can even remember. My mother gave me my first Toni home permanent when I was nine months old. I am sure my mother hoped this new product would give some manageability to my uncooperative tresses, which, even when pulled back in a ponytail until my eyes stretched, still slipped defiantly from rubber bands. Natural curl and a later fashion for straight styles delivered my younger sisters from my own youthful succession of stinking, stinging perms. But my hair was so fine, the intended curl often would not take, or, at the other extreme, would become a ball of frizz. No matter how tightly I held a towel over my eyes, the reeking fumes seeped through. Burning permanent solution dripped around my face, my neck wrenched over the sink as the prescribed minutes ticked off the kitchen timer. My mother and I suffered watering eyes and twitching noses in the vain hope that something could be done with that limp and hopeless hair. Persistently optimistic, we always imagined that this time the resulting curls would resemble those illustrated on the box. As I grew older, the mess was relegated to beauty parlor trips, where its smell persisted.

Perhaps the whole effort was an improvement, however, over the perms my mother recalls. She and her own mother endured salon permanents from a frightening piece of equipment, which I once saw in a museum. From a metal unit resembling a hair dryer, multiple electrical cords dangled, each attached to a metal clamp. Hair was soaked with solution, rolled on metal rods, and attached to the machine's clamps. Electric current then heated the rollers to set the waves and marcels popular at the time. My mother remembers the smell of burning hair during processing, and fuzzy, fried ends. The irony of all this torture women have endured in pursuit of curl is that permanents are not permanent at all. At the most, they last a few months, when the entire distasteful process has to be repeated.

Fortunately, God's promises are more reliable than the intentions of some stylists or the photographs and descriptions of the do-it-yourself kit. When we are tempted to dwell on our lank deficiencies, when we find it a struggle to do what is right rather than expedient or self serving, when our attention seems stuck on insurmountable problems, even when we falter and fail, God promises help, resolve, hope, and renewal. "God is not a man, that he should lie, nor a son of man, that he should change his mind. Does he speak and then not act? Does he promise and not fulfill?" (Numbers 23:19). We find the answers to these questions in the stories of both the Old and New Testaments, which illustrate how God fulfills His promises to nurture, sustain, and forgive those He loves. Psalm 100:5 assures us, "The Lord is good and his love endures forever; his faithfulness continues through all generations." When our troubles seem unmanageable, God offers a truly permanent solution.

Walking Rightly

*O*ur anticipation of September's return to school was primed by a leathery aroma of the shoe store. Heavy metal contraptions duly measured our feet for growth. While we cast our vote for fashionable, Mother tactfully directed us to practical and durable. For many of my formative years, this meant saddle oxfords, the only substantial shoes which could accommodate the metal corrective plates which shaped my stance. I can still recall the exhilaration of my first pair of canvas tennis shoes. Mother was less concerned with the appearance of our shoes than with how we walked in them, how they supported and protected our growing feet. She knew how important it was that we develop lifelong habits and postures to keep us walking well.

Walking rightly is a continuous spiritual challenge. Among devoted disciples who walked many miles with Christ during his earthly ministry, was Simon Peter. Courageous and bold, often the spokesman for the group, Peter made great efforts to adhere to the ways his Teacher prescribed. But try as he might, Peter was not always successful in following in Jesus footsteps. Peter tried to walk on water like his Lord, but sank when he became fearful (Matthew 14:22-34). He tried to support Jesus during His difficult hours in the Garden of Gethsemane, but, like the rest of the disciples, he fell asleep (Matthew 26:36-45). He tried to be a faithful friend, but he denied Christ when his own safety was threatened (Matthew 26:69-75). Peter's failures do not surprise us. We recognize them as our own.

We want to believe God's promises that he will sustain us in every circumstance, but often we try to take matters into our own hands, finally remembering His assurances only when our own failed efforts have been exhausted. We attempt to be supportive of friends and family members, but often our own needs and interests take precedence. We intend to remain faithful to our Christian principles, but how easy it is to succumb to pressures and pleasures of the world around us.

Despite Peter's weaknesses, Jesus commissioned him to spread the gospel (John 21:15-19). He became a great apostle, preaching the good news even when his life was threatened, and ultimately, as tradition has it, becoming a martyr for Christ. Like Peter, we, too, are forgiven our failures and blessed by God: "But if we walk in the light, as he is in the light, we have fellowship with one another, and the blood of Jesus, his Son, purifies us from all sin" (I John 1:7). Shod in His assurances, we are strengthened to rely on God's help, to imitate His love, and to withstand assaults to our faith. "Those who hope in the Lord will renew their strength. They will soar on wings like eagles; they will run and not grow weary, they will walk and not be faint" (Isaiah 40:31).

Kept in Stitches

*P*ast the shop window draped in luxurious seasonal fabrics, the jingle of the shop bell and a sharp odor of dyes met our entrance. Trips to the fabric store required time. There were pattern books to browse; fabric to choose; yardage to measure; thread, buttons, and zippers to match. Mother guided our selection from rows of corduroy, poplin, broadcloth, twill; seersucker, gingham, jersey, chintz; lawn, batiste, voile, swiss; taffeta, charmeuse, brocade, chiffon—unfurling bolts, teaching us to distinguish texture and drape, and suit them to a pattern's style.

An accomplished seamstress, Mother could often be found at her sewing machine, keeping three style-conscious young women in stitches. For my sisters and me, she sewed perfectly pleated wool skirts, matching every plaid. She made coordinated blouses and jumpers, and fashionable dresses. She tailored jackets and suits, whose fit could never be duplicated by ready-to-wear. She knew our measurements intimately, adjusting and altering every garment to a personalized fit. She patiently pinned hems on our fidgeting forms (adjusting mini skirts to more modest lengths than we requested.) She created swimsuits, nightgowns, shorts, and slacks. School clothes, sportswear, church dress, prom gowns, and even my sister's wedding gown . . . nothing was beyond my mother's artistic talents. She clothed us with love for every occasion.

Our Lord similarly stitches the seams of our lives. He helps us to select appropriate patterns for our behavior. He teaches us to know his precepts and guides us in applying them. He coordinates our choices with His will. He knows our needs intimately and tailors His attentions to our circumstances. He tempers our impatience and fashions our lives with His good judgment. His designs are for all occasions of our lives. His attentions are not reserved for church or desperate hours. As the spool of our days unravels, He is always at work, sewing the thread of our lives into the beautiful apparel of redemption he has designed for us. "I delight greatly in the Lord; my soul rejoices in my God. For he has clothed me with garments of salvation and arrayed me in a robe of righteousness" (Isaiah 61:10).

The Smell of Mistake

*E*ach fall as I enter the classroom, the smell of chalk, scrubbed desks, and waxed floors spurs my enthusiasm for the new school term ahead. Since so much of learning takes place through the process of trying and erring, it is not surprising that my memories of earlier school days are bound in the aroma of correction.

Every student is familiar with the woody scent of pencils, the regular rubbing and brushing of crumbs which caused erasers to wear out long before their lead. I still associate the smell of chalk dust with the blackboard revision of sentence diagrams in elementary school. Often we received tests pungently damp with mimeograph solvent from teachers' fingers purpled by scraping typos.

In high school typing classes, we needed a light hand to avoid wearing holes in copies as we rubbed out mistakes with ink erasers. Correcting copies meant multiple headaches, scenting and smudging fingers with carbon. One typing class experience was indelible. As I leaned to set my books near the assigned typewriter before class, a bottle of dime-store fragrance tumbled from my purse, shattering on the classroom floor. Searing with adolescent embarrassment, I scurried to mop the puddle of scent and broken glass, as students arrived twitching their noses with loud refrains of "What is that smell!?" There was no concealing my clumsiness. The error literally reeked.

Erasable paper made correcting college papers easier, but its print often smeared. Then came the chemical smell of typewriter correction fluid, requiring patience to dry. More recently evolved methods of revision have fewer aromatic associations. Typewriter correction tape obscured errors with a few strike strikeovers. Now, with a simple key stroke, computers allow us to eliminate our mistakes entirely.

When it comes to my personal faults, that is the kind of forgiveness I desire. I don't want my sins excused, or allowed, or blinked at while God holds his nose. I don't want a residual black mark to remain indelible in the inventory of someone I have offended. I want no trace of my misguided efforts, no evidence of my failed attempts, no vestige of my inert intentions, no hint of the harm I caused, no suggestion of my inadequacies. I want my failings to be blotted from memory, completely purged. And this is God's promise in Isaiah 1:18: "Though your sins are like scarlet, they shall be as white as snow."

Global Whirring

*E*ach morning in elementary school, we paused from our studies for a milk break. In the little red and white waxed carton was the distinctive smell of dairy and the cool pleasure of whole white milk, which revived us till lunch. While the teacher often took the moment to step out of the room, one rascal could not resist giving the globe at the front of the room a wild, surreptitious spin. The globe would clatter to the floor, rolling and banging, usually retrieved just in the nick of time as the teacher returned. Over the years, the battered ball began to look rather tattered: small chunks of Siberia were missing, Greenland had some gouges, and Peru was beginning to peel. The world was certainly not what it once had been.

I think of that schoolroom globe when the world begins to feel as though it is spinning out of control. We may feel our sentiments expressed in the title of a Broadway musical popular some years ago: "Stop the World I Want to Get Off." We may not really want to get off the globe exactly; we simply wish its spin would decelerate. Its speed makes us anxious. My parents cautioned us as children that our wish for the faster progress of days—to grow up, to wear make-up, to drive, to leave home, to get a job—would too soon become a desire for a slower pace of years. As we hustle through daily hassles, their predictions appear to have been fulfilled. Some days we feel we have more to do than we can possibly accomplish, we try to handle multiple demands at once, we flop into bed exhausted at the end of harried days and rise tired in the morning.

Our wild, frantic spin does seem to be doing some damage to the world as we used to know it. Headlines remind us daily of the toll our haste is taking on family relationships, human kindness, our environment, and spiritual purpose. Solutions to reduce the frenzy are not always easy. Demands of family, work, relationships, church, and self are unlikely to diminish. How can we choose which, among those worthy claims on our time, deserve our attentions?

Often we feel frazzled because we spend our hours merely reacting to current crises clamoring for attention. To maintain control of our time, we would be wise to re-evaluate often whether our days are being spent purposefully or frittered away. How many involvements are truly necessary? Why are they important? What could be postponed or delegated, or ignored? What are our true motivations for our expenditures of time? How worthy a determinant is self-interest in the choices we make? Who is in greatest need of our attentions at the moment? When is the most productive time to attend to our varied requirements? How much time do frivolous matters really require? Why are we hurrying through the satisfactions of our current engagements? What are we sacrificing in our frenetic activity? What long term effects will our choices have?

While we worry that we do not have enough time, we often spend it as though we had plenty, letting the coin of hours spill from our pockets. If we are wishing for an extra day in a week, a careful evaluation of how we budget our time is worthwhile. Once we have judiciously edited our expenditures of time, we can begin to adjust to a slower rhythm, to savor individual moments. Ecclesiastes 3:1 reminds us that "There is a time for everything, and a season for every activity under heaven." God gives us an established number of hours each day. He can help us determine priorities and then to give those choices our full attention, until we hear the insistent whirring of the world recede, and find the time to pause for a milk break.

Reading Riches

After tromping through snow shoveled against the curb where Mother had deposited me, I entered grand doors into the high-ceilinged ground-level vestibule, scented by the beauty salon which shared the building. Two flights of wide wood stairs led to the public library above, a peek of street visible from the landing's narrow window. The library itself was cavernous, great columns supporting a towering ceiling which dwarfed the tallest book cases. A formidable circulation desk anchored expanses of wood floor. Low-level children's books were to the right; non-fiction around the corner; an oak-cased card catalog, volumes of fiction, newspapers on wooden staves, and stereoscopes with accompanying historical slides to the left. Heavy tables dotted the perimeter against enormous windows with lazy street views. I could daydream there for hours, trying to study, and watching snowflakes grow. The room smelled of books, new and aging paper, dust, and furniture polish. Only rustling pages and whispers at circulation broke the contemplative silence.

What a remarkable concept a public lending library is. Access to a priceless collection of the world's great knowledge is available at no expense, not even a security deposit. With only a card registered in our name, we may read to our heart's content. And no matter how often we use that card, we will never exhaust all there is to learn. To this day, a library's rows and endless rows of books, the accumulated knowledge of all the volumes I shall never have time to read, inspire me with awe.

I am likewise daunted by the wisdom contained in the collected books of Scripture.

It is no surprise that the Bible remains consistently at the top of best seller lists today. Dramatic stories, history, law, genealogy, literature, poetry, speeches, letters, prayers, songs, prophecy, advice—its contents remain enthralling. No matter how reader-friendly the translation or how many times we have read it, the inspired Word of God continues to reveal its mysteries to us as long as we study it. Salvation comes, of course, to the simplest faith, but intellectual inquiry into spiritual questions can profoundly enrich that faith. Examining God's Word helps us to understand its complexities and discover its significance for our lives. Pondered by great minds, analyzed in endless commentary, the riches of The Good Book remain inexhaustible.

Yet, the apostle John tells us that the account we have in Scripture is incomplete: "Jesus did many other things as well. If every one of them were written down, I suppose that even the whole world would not have room for the books that would be written" (John 21:25). Imagine! The love of Jesus is so great that it cannot be entirely expressed by the limitations of human language and intellect. The Good News of God's grace gets better! Freely available, and claimed in our name at baptism, that grace will be gloriously elucidated when we come face to face with the living Word of God.

Cherished Correspondence

*W*hen we lived in Europe, an ocean away from family, my mother's regular letters often arrived on powdery scented stationery. Nothing transported me across the miles more poignantly than this soft suggestion of her own dulcet nature. Correspondence often carries scent and sentiment beyond the words themselves.

Inks have long spilled fragrance. Early Chinese ink sticks bore the scent of camphor and juniper seed oil, which was released when dampened. Indian ink bears the essence of patchouli, a plant used in its manufacture.

In eighteenth century England, Spanish leather storage cases scented writing papers with rose and violet. Perfumed stationery can easily be made by placing scented flowers or herbs, a fragrant sachet, or a magazine perfume strip into the box or drawer where writing papers and stationery are stored. Fragrant leaves or flowers may be tucked into envelopes as aromatic accompaniment to notes and letters.

The rarity of personal letters today makes them increasingly valuable. E-mail messages are quick and efficient, but disposable. In careless velocity, they can be excessively verbose or brusquely abrupt. They come, go, and are deleted. Letters, however, are a most personal gift. In the gestures of touching pen to paper, folding sheets into an envelope, licking the flap, hand addressing, applying the stamp, and dropping the missive into an often out-of-the way box, its recipient feels the caring touch. Letters can be held, carried, caressed, and reread. Even when ink has faded and paper has crumpled, old letters continue to convey the writer's heartfelt emotions and thoughts.

An elderly gentleman acquaintance allowed my husband and me to handle and read a valued family letter, which he had inherited. While we squinted and strained to read the beautifully fluent antique script, we could not miss the letter's heading: "Somewhere near Manassas." In reassurances of the writer's welfare and questions about home, we could feel a tingling transfusion of Civil War history pass up the arm as we held his endearing missive. We wondered at his fate in battle and that of his loved ones. The writer's words on the page remain a treasured legacy.

I recall the letters through which Mother kept in touch with us children when she was hospitalized. Her notes assured us of her nearness and promised her return. As I reflect now, I remember the remarkable discovery at that young age of the power of words to bridge absence through written communication.

It is expedient to simply call, but the phone can be a jangling and irritating interruption, its insistent immediacy an intrusion. And when the conversation is finished, I am often left feeling less than satisfied because we have discussed only the surface of matters as they presented themselves in the course of fast-paced conversation. The sequence of ideas is jumbled as we dart, divert, and digress from one topic to the next. There is little time for following-up on an idea when talk has moved to another subject. The speed of speech does not allow for formulating provocative questions or meaningful answers.

When we write, there are no anxious silences. We have time and space for thinking. Letters let us linger over matters which are important to us, selecting carefully the words and tone of what we wish to convey. We can tear them up and start over or elaborate in detail. We can rearrange, eliminate, or emphasize ideas to say exactly what we mean.

I have had the enduring privilege of faithful correspondence with a dear friend for many years. When a letter from her arrives, I tear into it in a rush, devour its contents, and then reread it at leisure later to savor detail, nuance, style, and wit. Our correspondence seldom relays day-to-day minutia, but the lag between letters allows us to identify and contemplate what has been particularly meaningful in our recent past. Personal reflections have deepened our friendship through the years. John Donne recognized the contribution of correspondence to relationships. He wrote, "More than kisses, letters mingle souls." Letters strengthen the bond between us by expressing interest in the lives of friends and loved ones while sharing our own concerns and enthusiasms.

Written correspondence is not only a means of maintaining relationships, it is also a manner of sorting through our own lives as we compose those letters, of arriving at realizations, of clarifying feelings and ideas for ourselves. The letters my friend and I exchange always bulge with clippings and enclosures, fodder for commentary and response in our next epistles. The acts of articulating our thoughts and finding personal applications illuminate our own views.

Prayer is, in effect, our spiritual correspondence with our unseen God. He asks us to communicate with Him often. "Pray in the Spirit on all occasions with all kinds of prayers and requests" (Ephesians 6:18). "Do not be anxious about anything, but in everything, by prayer and petition, with thanksgiving, present your requests to God" (Philippians 4:6). Too often, instead of steady correspondence with our Lord, we resort to prayer only in dire distress when all other human efforts have failed. But God wants to hear from us regularly.

He invites us to speak to Him about our own exultations and fears, to intercede for others. The location, posture, words of our prayers may vary to suit our circumstances. What is significant is that our spiritual sentiments are heartfelt and that we believe they will be answered. We receive God's reply in His Word, His answers evident in our lives and those for whom we pray.

In the gift of prayer, God assures us of His nearness. Whether spoken silently or aloud, prayer helps us to recognize our needs and blessings, inspiring solutions and gratitude. Our letters to our Lord strengthen the bonds of our relationship with Him. All we must do is send our prayers heavenward, sealed with faith, and wait for His marvelous response.

Church Dress

When we were children, our family occasionally worshipped at the little country church of my parents' youth. The simple white-frocked beauty stood on a breezy hilltop, her steeple a sparkling hat pin in stately millinery. Blue and green of sky and grass caught in her veils of colored glass, her cemetery a train of memories cascading to rolling farm fields beyond. Above the altar, Jesus stretched his hands in benediction from star-peaked spires of a heavenly kingdom, surely the paradise our Sunday school teachers promised. In her was a blessed, blissful quiet of whispered prayers, solemn cadences, familiar hymns.

Even on a hilltop, August breezes were faint. Hints of healthy perspiration, sweet perfume, and starched summer wear pulsed in the heat. Farm-callused hands in white gloves and Sunday cuffs paddled the air with paper fans picturing on one side Christ knocking at a door, and on the reverse a local funeral parlor advertisement. Organ notes melted overhead.

In the hot stillness, our family pressed together in narrow pews, sticky with old varnish. Sitting close, my sister and I fidgeted and smiled at private amusements in our light summer dresses—mine a pale green dotted swiss, my sister's a soft yellow voile embossed with velvety white flocked daisies. Mother kept us in beautiful stitches, handmade in tucked and ribboned detail. As we rustled our petticoats and shared some silliness which was about to escape into giggles, Mother's stern look suggested the impropriety of our motion and mirth. But her glance could do little to squelch our squirms or temper our tittering. We could hardly endure the heated hush a moment longer.

"The peace of God which passeth all understanding . . ." At those words, breath released, we bounced to our feet as the sermon ended. Twirling sideways after such restraint, I caught sight of our pew. ". . . keep your hearts and minds . . ." It was too much. I grabbed my praying sister's voile skirt and swung her around. Her eyes flew open to see behind us a fabulous daisy-flocked pew, where her warm dress had transferred its fuzzy blossoms. It looked as though the field flowers surrounding the church had been strewn indoors. We collapsed into heaps of crinoline in irrepressible merriment. And somehow, I think I heard the church herself flutter her skirts, laughing.

While this incident hardly demonstrates the propriety and solemnity services require, even on Sundays when we could not sit still, our parents were instilling in us the lifelong habit of church going. And while the practice lagged and sometimes lapsed during years of youthful independence, the strength of custom and a commitment to our faith compelled our return. Habit may seem questionable motivation for church attendance, but without grounding, a spiritual quest later in life may, like learning a foreign language as an adult, seem much less approachable, comfortable, or necessary. "Train up a child in the way he should go, and when he is old, he shall not depart from it" (Proverbs 22:6).

Manifest Mercy

*S*olemnly I kneeled at the altar, confessing my sins and preparing to receive the sacrament. Head bowed, I heard the words of blessing. Before my downcast eyes passed the white robes of ministers and dark, sensible shoes of elders distributing communion, when suddenly, bright pink toenails appeared before me, peeking from sandals of the clergy's young assistant. The jolt of unexpected color initially distracted me from meditation until I considered how God's mercy is often revealed to us in such surprising, earthbound ways. At that moment, in the taste, touch, sight, and smell of bread and wine, forgiveness came to us in human terms.

God did not remain in some remote heavenly realm, but came in human flesh to this world to redeem us, reminding us that we are to demonstrate His love to others. "This is how God showed his love among us: He sent his one and only Son into the world that we might live through him. This is love: not that we loved God, but that he love us and sent his Son as an atoning sacrifice for our sins. Dear friends, since God so love us, we also ought to love one another" (I John 4:9-11).

The elements of the Lord's Supper are not grain and grapes in their natural form, but rather this seed and fruit transformed by human hands into wine and bread as sacred sustenance for our souls. Thus God reveals His invisible grace to us in material form and conveys it through us to others in the forgiving word, the sympathetic touch, the consoling presence, the healing balm. His mercy is not reserved solely for the consecrated space of a church building or the reverent hours of worship; it is all about us in everyday manifestations, touching and infusing our humanity with holiness.

Sweating It Out

I really dislike sweating. Some find it invigorating, cleansing, cathartic, to exert such effort as to work up a lather. I would happily dispense with the dripping, smelling, and stinging eyes. A little glistening, as ladies' perspiring was once euphemistically termed, is quite sufficient, thank you.

Yes, I know all the benefits of a physical work-out to circulation, respiration, bone density, and good health, and I try my best to exercise semi-regularly, but I don't have to like it. As much that is good for us, I find morning walks a nuisance that impinges on time I would rather spend gardening, writing, cooking, reading, or almost anything else.

In spite of myself, once I get over the initial hurdle of propelling myself out the door, surprising pleasures often await. During the course of one week, I found a pocketful of change on the street, enough to post a letter to a friend. And I can follow the season's progression in neighbors' yards, like a fragrant jasmine which grows weekly to cover a mailbox in heady blossoms of greeting, or the astonishing aroma of mimosa as I arrive at the end of a block.

On one walk, huffing and puffing, I encountered a not-so-pleasant surprise—the putrid corpse of a decaying squirrel. The unexpected confrontation with the stench of death gave me sudden chills to contemplate the end of life and unsavory physical decomposition. Considering the irony that I was exerting myself to postpone just such ultimate fate, I turned the corner to encounter a sweet walk-side whiff of blazing red roses—life reaffirmed!

We hope to live long, healthy lives. We work at it—watch our diets, exercise, and avoid unwholesome habits. Although we know we cannot defy aging forever, we hope to keep our bodies functioning well and pain-free as long as possible. But we need not fear our demise when it inevitably arrives. Jesus reassures us that our physical death is not the end. When He met Mary coming to His tomb in the garden to anoint His body, "Jesus said to her, "I am the resurrection and the life. He who believes in me will live, even though he dies; and whoever lives and believes in me will never die" (John 11:25). As I stretch and walk, it is comforting to remember this assurance of life. Death? With faith, we don't have to sweat it!

Glancing Heavenward

he clean, damp breath of rain-washed air rolled in my car window. Limbs, branches, leaves, debris from the previous night's storm littered streets. I drove carefully, avoiding obstacles, when I saw standing in the open lawn of a corner church, a clergyman in ecclesiastical attire. Silhouetted against the revived green grass, hands shading his eyes, he looked to heaven. Evaluating the damage to the steeple? Wondering at the weather forecast? Thanking God for His refreshing rain? Contemplating eternity?

How seldom we cast our eyes heavenward. Intent on our daily demands, commonplace concerns, earthbound exigencies, and quotidian quests, we seldom consider what lies above and beyond us. Job 35:5 prompts us to "Look up at the heavens and see; gaze at the clouds far above you." Remember when we spent summer leisure imagining pictures in cloud formations, considering possibilities in patterns and shapes? It isn't always easy to figure out what God's plan is for us. Often it is because we are not looking to Him for answers, or because we are too attentive to momentary matters. Are we considering our purpose in the world, focusing on the hereafter? Perhaps it is time to glance heavenward again. "Trust in the Lord with all your heart and lean not on your own understanding" (Proverbs 3:5).

About the Author

Marsha Maurer has taught English with an emphasis on writing at colleges in the United States and Europe, currently at Augusta State University in Augusta, Georgia. She is the author of *In the Garden: A Collection of Prayers for Everyday*, published by Promise Press, an imprint of Barbour Publishing. Her writing and speaking are inspired by nature's invitation to spiritual reflection.